Front cover
The major types of 20th century Southwestern Indian jewelry are featured against a late 19th century Navajo woman's shawl. From left: traditional style Navajo silver squash blossom necklace, contemporary Zuni pendant of the "Sun God" kachina, silver concha belt by Roger Skeet, Jr., Santo Domingo jocla necklace, Hopi overlay pendant, and Zuni cluster pin by T. Mutte.

Library of Congress Catalog Number: 88-62164.
Library of Congress Cataloguing in Publication Data
Turnbaugh, William Arthur
Indian Jewelry of the American Southwest. Bibliography: p. 92.
Includes index.
1. Indians of North America—Southwest, Costume and adornment
2. Jewelry—Southwest. 3. Jewelry—Collectors and collecting.
I. Turnbaugh, Sarah Peabody, joint author. II. Title.
Printed in the United States of America.
ISBN: 0-88740-148-1
Published by Schiffer Publishing Ltd.
1469 Morstein Road, West Chester, Pennsylvania 19380

This book may be purchased from the publisher.
Please include $2.00 postage.
Try your bookstore first.

Contents

Foreword by Barry M. Goldwater 6

Preface and Acknowledgments 7

Indian Jewelry in History 8

Buying and Caring for Indian Jewelry 29

Navajo 40

Zuni... 50

Hopi 58

Rio Grande Puebloans 64

New Directions in Indian Jewelry 70

Gallery of Indian Jewelry 74

    Belts 74

    Bracelets 77

    Necklaces 79

    Pins... 84

    Rings 86

    Assorted Jewelry Styles 88

Glossary... 91

For Further Reading 92

Price Guide 93

Index.. 94

Turquoise, corn, and hot red chili peppers are the native South-western bounty spilling from this Hopi winnowing tray. The turquoise necklace is called a "tab necklace" due to the tab-shaped pieces of stone used to create it.

Prehistoric shell jewelry. The necklace of 295 beads and fetish-like pendants dates stylistically to the Mogollon culture, ca. 1000-1400 A.D. It is fashioned from Laevicardium *and* Spondylus *shell traded into the Southwest from the Gulf of California. The prehistoric bracelet of* Glycymeris *shell is from the Anasazi culture. It lacks the "umbo," or bump of shell along one edge, however, which is characteristic of most of these bracelets.*

Foreword

We who live in the Southwestern part of the United States owe a debt to our Indians that possibly never can be paid. We owe to them the culture and art that still dominates this part of the world.

When Spaniards and Mexicans first came here, they recognized the ability that the Indian peoples had with their hands and taught them how to use metal to make bracelets, earrings, and other items. It wasn't long until the Indians began using the silver pesos brought up from Mexico, and their jewelry started to grow from a silver beginning. They began to incorporate the turquoise from their own land into the ornaments they created. These products have become exceedingly popular, particularly in the last twenty years.

I collected Indian jewelry when anything over twenty-five dollars was a terribly high sum of money to pay. Those pieces that I had in my collection, which I passed on to my children, are now worth much more. But the greatest value of Indian jewelry is its intrinsic beauty. The Indians, with their cultural and artistic background, seem to give beauty to everything they touch.

BARRY M. GOLDWATER
Scottsdale, Arizona

Preface and Acknowledgments

For many, an item of Indian jewelry immediately brings to mind the American Southwest. Most who visit the region today, as in decades past, cannot resist selecting a special piece of Indian jewelry to take home as a remembrance of the gorgeous scenery and fascinating people. Turquoise and silver jewelry is worn and sold almost everywhere in the Southwest. It can be found at roadside stands, gift shops, high fashion galleries, trading posts, pawn shops, native craft cooperatives, and flea markets.

The seemingly endless sea of turquoise and silver looks all the same at first. What does one look for? Where is the best place to buy Indian jewelry? Is the metal sterling and the turquoise genuine? And, what is a fair price to pay?

Indian Jewelry has been written as an introduction for those whose interest is just beginning as well as for those already familiar with the Southwest and its native arts and crafts. It illustrates real handmade Indian jewelry that is readily available and within an affordable price range for the average buyer or collector. The guide includes very few one-of-a-kind designer pieces, which generally are much more expensive. It does picture a few examples of machine-made and mass-produced American or imported imitations in order to assist the reader in recognizing pieces that are not genuine handmade Indian work. The book follows the development of Indian jewelry from early times to the present day and distinguishes Navajo, Zuni, Hopi, and Pueblo styles from one another. Finally, it suggests what to look for when buying Indian jewelry, examines modern trends, and provides a guide to the prices of some examples.

Appreciation of a piece of Indian jewelry usually begins with its eye appeal. For many, though, a deeper enjoyment comes with recognizing the materials, the craftsmanship, the design, and the traditions that combine to make each piece unique.

Many people and institutions have shared their knowledge, time and collections with us to make this book possible. We thank each for their important contributions. We wish to thank the following individuals and institutions in particular for assistance: Bill Blass, Vincent Price, Jim Turpen and Tobe Turpen Trading Company of Gallup, Richardson Trading Company of Gallup, Linda Martin and Mesa Verde National Park, the Gilbert Ortega Galleries of Fine Indian Arts, the staff of Kingstown Camera, the officers and trustees of the Museum of Primitive Culture, Barbara Considine, Lisa Fiore, Paula Law, Louise Turnbaugh, Dr. and Mrs. Berkley Peabody, and Marion Houston.

WILLIAM A. TURNBAUGH
SARAH PEABODY TURNBAUGH

Anasazi jewelry from Mesa Verde, Colorado. All of these shell and turquoise objects—more than 2,000— came from one pouch which may have belonged to a prehistoric trader.

Indian Jewelry in History

"American Indian jewelry is indeed timeless and looks wonderful when worn with modern clothes—day or evening."

—Bill Blass, 1988

The American Southwest evokes many images. Deserts of sagebrush and cactus flowering in springtime. Navajo Indians herding sheep and weaving colorful wool rugs. Ten gallon hats, rawhide fringe, and tooled leather boots from the Wild West days of cowboys, gunslingers, and hanging judges. Bells pealing from Spanish missions. Roadside stands offering fry bread, home-grown apricots, and pinyon nuts. The burning bite of jalapeno pepper jelly. Plump loaves baked in outdoor ovens. Mesas and canyons shimmering in the still, dry heat and glare of reservation deserts. A rose and lavender sun setting behind pink adobe pueblos. Pungent mesquite smoke curling upward toward the first bright stars of evening. The distant howl of coyotes. Long ristras of dried red chili peppers. Blue corn tortillas. Tumbleweeds. Roadrunners and jack rabbits. Archaeological ruins. Indian rodeos and kachina dances. Pottery, rugs and baskets. Turquoise and silver jewelry.

Indian Jewelry! Perhaps of all the Southwestern images, turquoise and silver is the one most widely shared. Indian jewelry has been made for centuries; today it is created, worn, and sold almost everywhere in the Southwest. American fashion designer Bill Blass recently observed to us that "American Indian jewelry is indeed timeless and looks wonderful when worn with modern clothes—day or evening." We agree wholeheartedly. From ancient times to the present, Indian jewelry has been a uniquely American art form. The fact that it can be worn as well as admired and enjoyed only adds to its appeal. Today, the people of the Southwest wear turquoise and silver jewelry naturally and gracefully in their everyday activities. Bold concha belts, bead necklaces, bracelets, rings, and pins accessorize all styles of clothing from casual to elegant. The fashionable streets of Santa Fe and Scottsdale explode with it, as do aisles of Southwestern supermarkets. Even young babies held in their mothers' arms often are adorned with tiny turquoise earrings and silver bracelets.

This ring, resting on an ancient grinding tool called a mano, is an example of recycling. The drilled turquoise stone is an archaeological tab pendant from the Anasazi culture. It probably dates to Pueblo II (900-1100 A.D.) times. Yet, an early 20th century artisan retrieved the stone from desert sands and set it in this plain Navajo-style silver bezel and split shank ring.

Prehistoric Stone and Shell Work

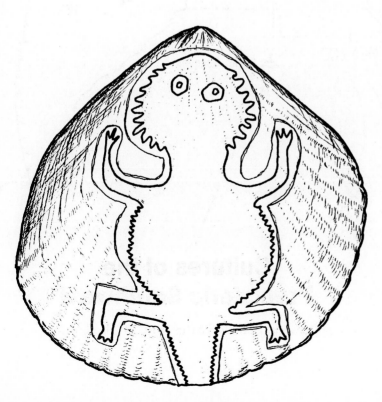

Turquoise frog pendant, Anasazi culture, Mesa Verde, Colorado.

Jewelry has been worn in the Southwest since prehistoric times. Although styles have changed through the centuries and Southwestern native American metalsmithing of iron, brass, and silver has been learned only within the past 200 years, many of the modern styles of Indian jewelry retain elements from the earlier traditions that preceded them.

Exactly when jewelry making became a regular activity in Southwestern cultures remains undetermined. Drilled shell, bone, stone and turquoise beads, for example, have been created in the Southwest for thousands of years. More elaborate pieces—small carved figures of animals and birds, as well as shell bracelets and turquoise mosaic work—also have been made through many centuries.

In the past two millenia, three major prehistoric cultures—the Hohokam, Mogollon, and Anasazi—created much early jewelry. Each of these cultures was ancestral to some contemporary tribes living in the Southwest. The Hohokam preceded the Pima and Papago of southern Arizona, the Anasazi were the forerunners of modern-day Pueblo tribes of Arizona and New Mexico, and some Mogollon and Anasazi may have been ancestors of the contemporary Zuni.

Etched horned toad on Laevicardium *shell, Hohokam culture, Snaketown, Arizona.*

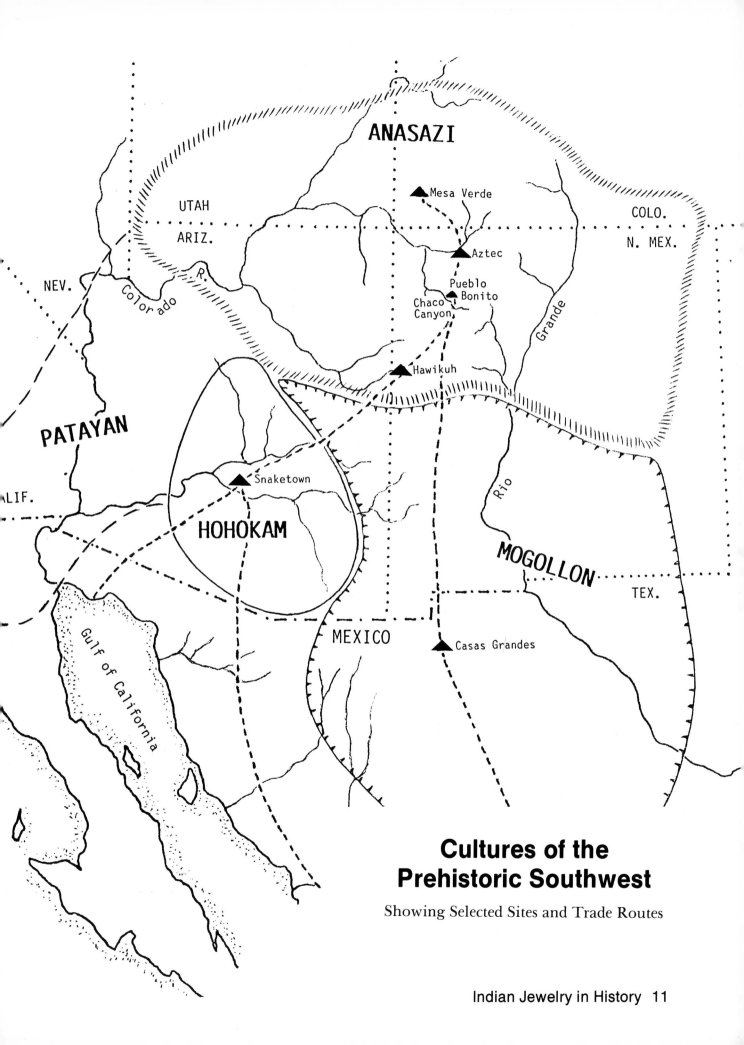

Cultures of the Prehistoric Southwest

Showing Selected Sites and Trade Routes

Pueblo Bonito archaeological site, Chaco Canyon, Arizona. The prehistoric Anasazi culture began to build this D-shaped complex of rooms in about 800 A.D. The extensive settlement at Chaco Canyon probably served as a turquoise processing center between about 900-1200 A.D. During this time, Chaco Canyon was located on a major turquoise trade route that extended from the Santa Fe area to Mesoamerica via Casas Grandes in Mexico. Archaeologists have excavated tens of thousands of turquoise artifacts from the many ruins in Chaco Canyon. The source of most of this turquoise was the Cerrillos mines south of Santa Fe, New Mexico. This turquoise was traded to Toltec and Aztec peoples in Mesoamerica in return for salt, brightly colored macaw feathers, unusual shells, and other goods.

Cliff Palace, Mesa Verde, Colorado. Cliff Palace is the largest and the best-known of the Anasazi cliff dwellings at Mesa Verde (Spanish for "green table" or "green mesa"). The Anasazi built Cliff Palace in the 13th century A.D. More than 200 rooms and 24 kivas are tucked away under the cliff in this dwelling.

Prehistoric trade routes that followed major drainages of the Southwest and ran along the mountainous foothills crisscrossed the Southwest through thousands of years. These footpaths were travelled by traders who made exotic goods available to each of these early cultures. Some of the materials found their way into jewelry making. Sometime after 700 A.D. a general trade route was formed that connected western Mexico and the Gulf of California with the Hohokam settlement of Snaketown, located to the southeast of present-day Phoenix, Arizona. In the 11th century A.D. another major trade route extended northward from southern Mexico through Casas Grandes in Chihuahua, Mexico, to the Anasazi settlement of Chaco Canyon in New Mexico. The sites of Snaketown and Chaco Canyon are among the most significant and largest in the Southwest. In general, marine shells like abalone, spiny oyster, and olivella moved northward from the coast, along with other goods that probably included copper bells, brightly colored macaw feathers, salt, and domesticated maize or corn. Goods including raw materials like turquoise as well as finished jewelry and textiles were among the items that travelled from the Southwest into Mexico.

Cultural ideas were exchanged as well, which accounts in part for similarities in architectural styles, pottery and basketry designs, religious concepts, and other traits between the cultures of the Southwest and northern Mexico.

Many of the early pre-European traditions survived into historic times despite a number of challenges. Two significant stresses were an increase in the area's population and a shortage of arable land and water. Increased population prompted continuous raids and warfare. And the severe drought between 1276 and 1299 further strained the already scarce natural resources of the arid Southwest. These types of pressures led to an abandonment of most major sites before the 14th century A.D. Many people relocated along more secure water supplies such as the valley of the Rio Grande. It was in this valley in the 16th century that the Spanish encountered most of the puebloans when Coronado and the Spanish *conquistadores* travelled north out of Mexico after arriving in the New World.

Since prehistoric times, decoration has been important to the native inhabitants of the Southwest. This ornamental green band was added to the stonework of a wall at Aztec National Monument (1100 A.D.) for purely aesthetic interest.

Spanish Contact and Development of Silversmithing

When the Spanish entered the Southwest, they were looking for the elusive wealth and treasure of the "Seven Cities of Cibola." After failing to find vast stores of treasure and precious jewels or streets paved with silver and gold, they took control of the new land and its inhabitants. By 1582, the Spanish had gained firm control of the Southwest. The Indians lost their lands to Spanish settlers, soldiers, and missionaries. They were ordered to pay taxes to the Spanish, and they were enslaved and forced to adopt Christianity. Thousands of Indians died from European diseases to which they had no natural resistance. Spanish rule lasted until 1821, broken only briefly during the Pueblo Revolt of 1680-1692. During this interlude, the Indians temporarily succeeded in driving out the Spanish and wresting their lands back. In 1821, rule of the region shifted to Mexico. Then, in 1848, the Southwest territory passed to the United States as a result of the Mexican War. During the Spanish colonial period, traditional native jewelry making generally declined. Cultural fragmentation, triggered by increased mortality rates due to disease and warfare and new religious, social and economic stresses disrupted the old ways. Although the use of turquoise still remained popular after 1600 A.D., jewelry was made less frequently. That which was created was not very elaborate or well made. Mosaic work and inlay declined, and stones and shells were seldom carved. Yet, among some Rio Grande pueblos—Hopi, Zuni, and Acoma—work with turquoise, shell and other materials continued, although at a more subdued level.

Nineteenth century Mexican blacksmiths taught Navajos to make iron horse bits and to work with silver. This Spanish Colonial style iron horse bit was used in the American Southwest. All of the hand-forged techniques with which it is decorated—punch work, chisel work, file work, and stamping—found their way into early American Indian silver working in the Southwest. (Compare silver ketoh, page 25.)

*Mosaic jewelry fro[m]
the pueblos of the R[io]
Grande valley, ear[ly]
1980's. The mosa[ic]
techniques used he[re]
by Florence Aguilar [of]
Santo Domingo Pueb[lo]
to create the penda[nt]
and by Charlot[te]
Reano (left) and
Manuelita Flower [of]
Cochiti Pueblo (righ[t])
for the earrings a[re]
modern interpretatio[ns]
of one of the m[ost]
ancient and traditio[nal]
methods that R[io]
Grande puebloans ha[ve]
used to fashion nat[ive]
Southwestern jewel[ry].
The mosaic overl[ay]
consists of bl[ue]
turquoise, black j[et]
and white clam moth[er]-
of-pearl. The beauti[ful]
orange shell [is]
Spondylus, or spi[ny]
oyster. Beads and fra[g]-
ments of this sh[ell]
have been excavated
along with turquoise
at many sites throug[h]-
out the Southwest. [In]
early times, Spondy[lus]
shell was brought in[to]
the Southwest alo[ng]
established native tra[de]
routes stretching fro[m]
the California co[ast]
and Sea of Cortez [or]
the Gulf of Califor[nia]
to Arizona and N[ew]
Mexico.*

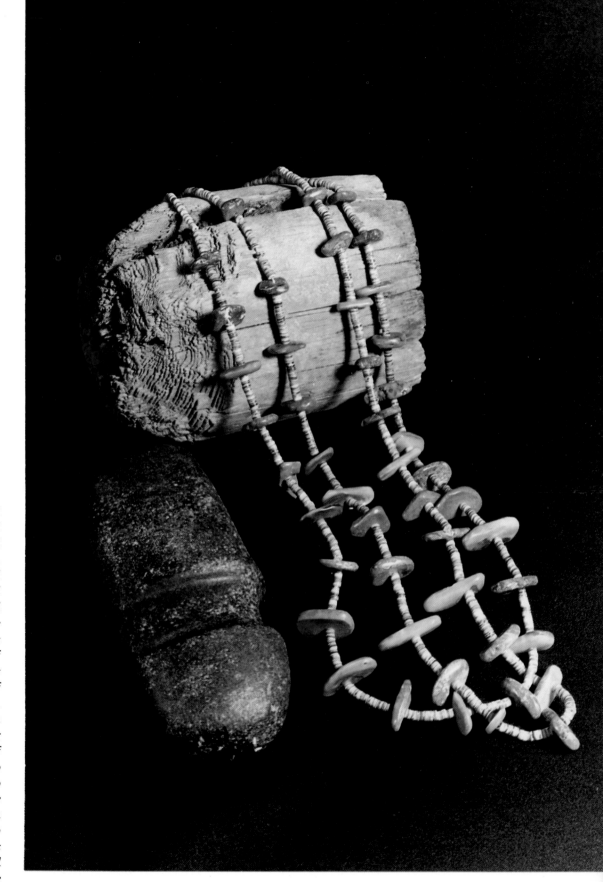

This two-strand necklace was created by combining shell heishi beads with tabular turquoise and red abalone shell beads. Although all Indian peoples of the Southwest wear this popular type of necklace, it usually is made by puebloans of the Rio Grande valley. The puebloans, in turn, trade it—along with other types of beads—to the Navajo and western pueblo peoples. Red abalone shell has been used in Southwestern jewelry since prehistoric times when it was obtained through trade from the Gulf of California.

Meanwhile, Spanish and Mexican influence on the Navajo and Pueblo cultures was strong. The native peoples were especially intrigued with the Spanish horses and their decorative silver bridles and ornaments, and Native Americans gradually acquired some of their own through trade or raids. Through the 18th and early 19th centuries, the Spanish traded metal implements and jewelry to the Navajo and Puebloans. Iron, copper, brass, and silver objects soon became familiar possessions. However, it appears that the natives were not working metal themselves during this time. The earliest pieces of metal worked by natives living in the Southwest probably were iron bits for horse bridles that Navajo and Zuni were learning to make in the second quarter of the 19th century, after the Southwest had passed from Spanish to Mexican rule.

This early rocker-engraved ring of coin silver probably was made at Zuni between 1880 and 1885. The Spanish brought metal rings as trade goods to the Southwest until the third quarter of the 19th century when the Navajo learned silversmithing. The technique of rocker engraving passed from the Plains Indians to the Navajo who, in turn, taught the decorative method to the Zuni in about 1880.

Early trade goods, ca. 1550-1875. A wide variety of goods was traded to native Americans during the earliest years of contact with European explorers and traders. Trade introduced new wares into Indian societies all over North America. Some of the merchandise included wrought iron beaver traps, firearms and equipage, metal knives, colorful cotton and woolen fabrics, glass beads, clay smoking pipes, and coins. Explorers and traders as well as missionaries introduced Christianity, too, to native America.

Just as Mexico assumed control of the region in 1821, the Santa Fe Trail was blazed between Independence, Missouri, and Santa Fe. Traveling Mexican silversmiths, called *plateros* (from the Spanish word for silver, *plata*), and blacksmiths created quantities of metal objects for the lively trade that followed. By the 1830's men had learned the basics of blacksmithing and were recycling worn-out brass and copper utensils into bracelets, crosses, and other ornaments. The first Navajo to learn iron working was Atsidi Sani, who persuaded a Mexican smith working near Mount Taylor to teach him the skill in about 1850. Not until later in the century did native silversmithing begin. (See the Navajo chapter below for further discussion.)

This Navajo silversmith sits at his anvil where he is fashioning hand-wrought silver jewelry.

Native silversmiths used various methods to work silver. Several major techniques are illustrated here, including hammering, filing, die stamping and casting.

Coin necklace and bracelet, mid 20th century. Jewelry that incorporates coins—and especially the coin necklace—was created from about 1895-1925. Undefaced coins again were used with great popularity in the 1940's-1950's and in the 1970's. This bracelet was made sometime after 1921, which is the date on the Morgan silver dollar. The necklace post-dates 1945, the date on its most recent coin. The naja is considerably earlier, dating to ca. 1870-1880.

Opposite page:
Catalog and price list of J. Lorenzo Hubbell, Arizona Indian Trader, 1905. This booklet gives descriptions and prices of coin silver jewelry shortly after the Navajo began to create it on a regular basis for commercial sale to off-reservation markets.

Classic Period of Indian Jewelry Making

Prior to about 1850, the Navajo and Pueblo peoples acquired their silver ornaments through trade or warfare with Spanish settlers or Mexican plateros. Some also came from neighboring Plains Indians who had acquired trade silver from English, French, and American sources. As the Navajo, Zuni, Hopi, and Rio Grande puebloans began to work silver later in the century, they turned to coins as a ready source of the metal. American coins were worked into jewelry prior to 1890; thereafter defacing a U.S. coin was outlawed. Mexican pesos were substituted up until 1930 when their export to the American Southwest was forbidden. Sterling silver ingots with a slightly purer silver content replaced the coins. Around 1935, sterling silver in convenient sheets and wire forms became increasingly available from Indian traders. Today, the majority of Indian jewelry is still made using sheet and wire.

Turquoise, a traditional favorite with native Americans, was first combined with silverwork around 1880. Between 1895 and 1900 the Indian trader Don Lorenzo Hubbell capitalized on the popularity of the bright blue stone by importing Persian turquoise for trade to the Navajo. After 1900 the local supply of turquoise increased as more mines were opened in the Four Corners region.

Navajo Silverware and Jewelry

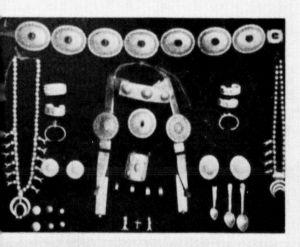

All these productions of the Navajo silver-
h are from coin silver, melted, hammered or
led with their own primitive appliances. Some
finished with plain surface, others are elab-
ly engraved, stamped or embossed in designs
dless variety.

r belts (belt plates round and oval) . . . .
. . . . $30.00 to $40.00

r mounted bridles . . . . $30.00 to $40.00

ow spherical beads, various sizes, per string
. . . . $10.00 to $35.00

r Conchas for ladies' belt buckles, per ounce
. . . . $1.25 to $1.75

r bracelets with matrix turquoise, according
color and size of stone . . . . $2.25 to $10.00

r bracelets without settings, per ounce . . . . . .
. . . . $1.25 to $1.75

r finger rings, matrix turquoise settings, ac-
rding to color and size of stones . . $1.25 to $5.00

Silver finger rings without turquoise . . . .
. . . . $0.25 to $1.50

Silver buttons . . . . $0.15 to $1.00

Silver pendants, each $1.00

Silver spoons with matrix turquoise settings, price according to size and color of stones.
Each . . . . $3.50 to $5.00

Silver spoons, arrow and Indian head design on handle, per doz . . . . $8.00 to $18.00

Moqui Pottery

Jars, vases, basins, canisters of almost every characteristic aboriginal model and emblematic decoration, from . . . . $0.25 to $5.00

Navajo cooking pots, also used as drums in ceremonial dances . . . . $0.50 to $1.50

By the early 20th century the making of silver and turquoise jewelry was widespread. Earliest pieces were created in simple styles and techniques adapted from the Spanish, Mexican, and Plains peoples. Domed buttons, silver beads, horse bridles, simple loop earrings, bracelets, and rings were among the first creations. Belts of conchas, squash blossoms and najas for necklaces and horse headstalls, ketohs (or men's bow guards), and manta pins followed. The bold, plain silverwork of this early jewelry occasionally was decorated with simple engraved, stamped, filed, or chiselwork designs formed with hand-made tools. More complicated silverworking techniques such as applique came later.

Indian trader tokens, ca. 1865-1935. The late 19th to early 20th century Indian trading post played an important role in providing a commercial outlet for Indian-made goods. Many Indian traders paid native artisans with tokens for their jewelry, rugs, baskets, or other handicrafts. The craftsmen then could use the tokens as needed to purchase foodstuffs and other supplies that the trading post stocked.

Opposite page:
Early ketoh or bow guard for protecting the wrist, ca. 1890-1920. Modern examples are worn by men for ceremonial occasions only. This silver ketoh is set with a hand-ground turquoise cabochon. The silverwork was done using the same punched, stamped, and filed techniques that are found on earlier 19th century Southwest iron and silverwork. This ketoh has been remounted on a more recent leather backing. Domed buttons dating to the early 20th century have been sewn along the sides of the ketoh to add decorative interest.

Pueblo Indians selling crafts at a railroad stop, ca. 1900. The railroads brought tourists to the Southwest, and tourists attracted native vendors to the railroad stops. The existence of this economic outlet greatly influenced the commercial development of native silversmithing, rug weaving, and basketry and pottery making in the early 20th century.

Early coin silver jewelry examples, typical of the late 19th century. The early Navajo or Zuni style bracelet features simple chiselwork and stamped designs including "end-of-file" decoration. An oval stone with plain bezel attached to a sunburst-style silver plate and other details of manufacture—as well as some visible wear—suggest an early date of about 1880-1900 for this bracelet. The early Navajo style naja probably dates to about 1870-1880. It is all handmade and decorated with cold chisel-stamping along the inner edge of the interior crescent and arrow point. The loop on this naja is very heavily worn; it may have been attached originally to a headstall for a horse. Currently, the naja is strung on a strand of silver beads dating to the 1930's or 1940's.

This early jewelry synthesized native and non-native jewelry making traditions by blending ancient stoneworking techniques of early puebloans with native silverworking influenced by Spanish and Plains Indians and taught by Mexican smiths. Today, these pieces are considered the "classic" jewelry of the American Southwest. Silverwork of individual tribes and regions was not yet distinguishable, while Mexican, Spanish and Plains Indian influences could be readily discerned. These products were created by Indians for their own use.

The availability of turquoise and silver, together with better silverworking tools, enabled craftsmen to supply the growing market among Indian traders and tourists who were arriving in droves by railroad to visit the Southwest. The entry of women into the craft was one measure of its rapid commercialization. Although silversmithing originally was practiced by men, Navajo women were working the metal by 1918.

Fred Harvey, among others, played a major role in promoting Indian jewelry to tourists at railroad stops, concessions, and his chain of Harvey hotels through the Southwest. Many pieces of older Indian jewelry that may be found today in flea markets, attics, and shops throughout the country are the distinctive "Harvey House" style examples that date to that period when Indian jewelry was first commercialized and made more widely available to tourists. Though made by Indians, much of this jewelry was fashioned in workshops which used thinner silver, lower quality stones and design motifs created to appeal to the popular conception of "Indian-ness."

Meanwhile, through the early 20th century, the "classic" style of jewelry gradually diverged into clearly recognizable modern-day styles associated with Navajo, Zuni, Hopi and Rio Grande puebloans. More recently, these distinctions have again begun to blur as native artisans redefine the tradition and move toward a contemporary, more universal or pan-Indian art form called "new Indian" jewelry by one of its founders, the Hopi artist Preston Monongye.

Shops and galleries such as Hopi House on the South Rim of the Grand Canyon offer a wide range of Indian jewelry for sale. Hopi House, founded by Fred Harvey in about 1905, is a recreation of a Hopi Indian pueblo. It was designed for Harvey by the famous architect Mary Colter.

Early 20th century firms—like the Fred Harvey Company, Maisel, and Sun-Bell—that made inexpensive jewelry are credited with keeping white interest in native jewelry alive through the Great Depression. The copper bracelet with silver applique sunburst design and the naja earrings are early products of these firms. They have some handwork to them, though they are mostly machine-made. The three rings date to the 1970's and are recent examples of low cost sterling silver and turquoise jewelry which companies like Bell still make today.

These early 20th century Harvey House style bracelets are decorated with innovative die stamping including arrows, snakes, and suns that looked "Indian" and readily appealed to tourists. These examples are partly handmade and partly machine-made and were mass-produced by Indian employees of the Fred Harvey Company. Tourist-era jewelry of the early 1900's was sold as curios at railroad stations, roadside stops, and the large hotels and curio shops at tourist centers. This jewelry is much lighter in weight and less expensive than that made non-commercially for native use. Harvey House jewelry is highly collectible today.

Buying and Caring for Indian Jewelry

"The flavor of the West is half the fun of collecting."
—Bob Ward, Original Indian Trading
Post, Santa Fe, 1976

People buy Indian jewelry for many different reasons. Some simply enjoy wearing the bold, bright accessories. Others are fascinated with the American Indian heritage and traditions that the jewelry represents. Still others buy high quality, handmade Indian jewelry as a financial investment.

The interests of collectors are as varied as the collectors themselves. Some collections are eclectic and include articles of many types. Other collections concentrate in different specific areas. For example, one person may prefer to collect only Zuni cluster jewelry, while another may acquire as many different varieties of the "squash blossom" necklace as possible. Another collector may purchase only examples of Indian jewelry that are set with high-grade spiderweb turquoise from various mines. Some may emphasize early pieces from the 19th century while others concentrate on examples of "new Indian" jewelry. Whatever their interests, collectors should always remember to buy only what they truly like. Any American Indian piece that is handmade with workmanship and materials of high quality will always give its owner much enjoyment and personal satisfaction.

Opposite page:
Peering into the pawn vault of Tobe Turpen's Trading Company in Gallup, New Mexico, is a breath-taking experience! (Photo courtesy of Jim Turpin.)

Jewelry may be purchased directly from Indians at roadside stands like this example, located near the Little Grand Canyon on the Navajo Reservation near Cameron, Arizona.

Where to Buy Indian Jewelry

Indian jewelry is sold by many types of vendors in the Southwest. It may be purchased directly from Indians on reservations and in pueblos, or from traveling Indians selling at flea markets or in cities such as Santa Fe and Albuquerque, at reservation trading posts, in pawn shops located in towns close to reservations, at native craft guilds and cooperatives, in elegant shops and galleries in larger cities, and at souvenir shops, convenience stores, and gas stations throughout the Southwest. Care should be taken in making a selection. Good quality turquoise and silver jewelry that is handmade by American Indians may be mixed in with a selection of imitations, such as similar-looking non-Indian jewelry, Asian copies, or plastic "turquoise" and nickel silver pieces with no silver content. Even articles purchased directly from native Americans are not always completely handmade. When purchasing Indian jewelry, one should rely on dealers who have a good reputation. Local chambers of commerce, museums, tribal crafts guilds, and native cooperatives will give potential buyers the names of trustworthy shops and dealers in the area. A free source directory of native American owned and operated businesses is also available by writing to the Indian Arts and Crafts Board, Room 4004, U.S. Department of the Interior, Washington, DC 20204.

The Hopi First Mesa village of Sichomovi. Most of these houses shelter craftsmen who make and sell jewelry, baskets, pottery, and kachinas in their homes. Many of the artists readily welcome potential buyers.

Looking west along the Palace of the Governors, Santa Fe, New Mexico. Each day, Indian artisans gather at the portals of the picturesque Palace of the Governors, where they sell jewelry to tourists and passersby. The Indian vendors who are privileged to display their wares at this location are selected periodically in a lottery. (Photo by Robert N. Lynch.)

Opposite page:
Even a surprise snowstorm in early May does not discourage buying and selling of Indian jewelry at an impromptu road-side stand near Flagstaff, Arizona.

Indian jewelry is available in many well-appointed galleries in major Southwestern cities. Inset: Mr. Gilbert Ortega offers a wide selection in his many stores in Arizona and New Mexico. (Inset photo by Gerald Duduyer, courtesy of Gilbert Ortega Galleries of Fine Indian Arts).

Hubbell Trading Post, Ganado, Arizona. The Hubbell Trading Post is the oldest operating trading post on the Navajo Reservation. It began in the 1870's and is now a national historic site while still functioning as a traditional trading post with a grocery store and pawn counter.

Pawn shops such as Richardson's Trading Company in Gallup, New Mexico, are worth a visit when looking for a special piece of Indian jewelry to purchase.

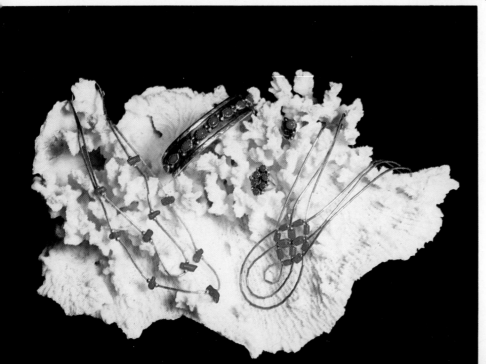

This nugget of natural turquoise from Royston, Nevada, is encircled with silver applique leaf or feather elements. This popular form may be worn either as a pendant or as a pin.

How to Buy Indian Jewelry

Consumers should educate themselves before spending a significant amount of money on Indian jewelry. By reading books and magazine articles on Indian jewelry and by viewing jewelry collections in museums, galleries, and shows, a collector soon will acquire a "feeling" for jewelry of genuine, handmade Indian workmanship. When examining a piece of jewelry, collectors should look at the stone, the metal, and the quality of workmanship.

The Stone

Turquoise is a hydrous aluminum phosphate with a hardness of 5 to 6 on the Moh scale of 1 to 10. Copper salts deposited in the stone give it the distinctive blue-green color. The rock in which turquoise is found is sometimes called the "mother rock." Veins or spots of this rock which show up as markings in turquoise are called "matrix." Black matrix includes the minerals manganese, iron or silver, while brown matrix is colored by the presence of iron oxide or copper. White matrix consists of white quartz or silica. Turquoise is mined in many different areas of the Southwest, as well as elsewhere around the world. It comes in many different shades of blue and green; a single mine often produces a variety of colors of stone and matrix. Nuggets or "seafoam" turquoise may be used in jewelry in virtually a natural state. Or, turquoise may be carved, shaped into flat tabs, polished into round or oval cabochons, or drilled and ground into rolled turquoise beads or heishi.

Not all turquoise is natural. Often, it is difficult to tell whether a stone's color is true, the matrix real, and the quality of the stone good.

Examples of red coral and silver jewelry spill across white coral from the Pacific. Red coral is a popular material for use in Indian jewlery. Test for coral: A drop of lemon juice placed on an inconspicuous spot on coral will effervesce or bubble slightly if the coral is genuine. The two red coral and liquid silver necklaces were hand-assembled by Southwestern Indians. But the Mediterranean coral probably was drilled and polished in Italy before export to the Southwest. The liquid silver beads are a machine-made import. The bracelet and rings are all handmade.

ndian jewelry uses native Southwestern stones other han turquoise, including agatized petrified wood rom Arizona. Cut petrified wood cabochons were specially popular in jewelry made in the 1930's- *1940's and again in the 1970's. A bracelet with an oval cabochon of picture jasper from Utah (front left) is included here for comparison.*

Turquoise may be dyed or may be stabilized with plasticizing epoxy, resin, oils or waxes— specially if it was a low grade or soft stone in its natural state. Turquoise also may be reconstituted using powdered turquoise and an epoxy or plastic. Reconstituted turquoise or block turquoise has been made since the 1930's, and the technologies used today are so complex that it is often almost impossible to tell whether a stone is natural or reconstituted. Spiderweb matrix in turquoise is often created today in block form.

Some simple tests for the authenticity of a stone do exist. They include:

Hot Needle Test. If the tip of a hot needle only chars the turquoise, it probably is a natural stone. If it chars and melts the stone, then the stone is either stabilized with plasticizing materials or the stone is not genuine.

Knife Scratch Test. A steel knife blade usually will scratch turquoise. If the scratch edges look ragged under magnification, then the stone probably is real. If the edges look smooth, the stone is stabilized.

Ultraviolet Light Test. Turquoise that has been plasticized often fluoresces.

Naturally, it is impractical to perform most of these tests before purchasing an item, so the best advice is to deal with someone who is trustworthy when buying Indian jewelry. In addition, other stones including jade, variscite, chrysocolla, malachite, dyed howlite and odontolite, blue sodalite and lapis lazuli, as well as reconstituted or block turquoise may be used instead of natural stone and are sometimes confused with the genuine article. Other materials that are occasionally used include coral, petrified wood, picture jasper, mother-of-pearl, shell, jet, ivory, and ironwood.

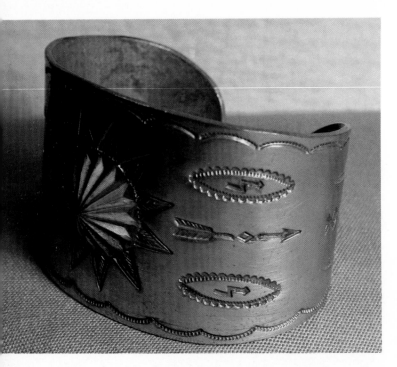

This Navajo-style copper bracelet is hand worked, with embossing, filing, and stamping. It probably dates to the early 20th century. Close examination of the metal's surface near the designs reveals the workman's lightly scribed guidelines. The bracelet was made for the early tourist trade in the Southwest.

Wrought concha pin (reverse). To tell whether a piece of jewelry is really hand-wrought, examine the back of it. As shown here, pounded or hand wrought silver usually will have tiny stress marks. On the other hand, machine-made jewelry often will look smooth. The four scars near the center of this piece are old solder marks which reveal that this concha has been recycled. It originally may have been worn as a slide on a concha belt and probably had two copper slides or loops attached at these points.

The Metal

Handmade Indian jewelry usually is fashioned using hand wrought (hammered and/or cut) or hand cast techniques. It may be ornamented in various ways, including filework, chiselwork, or stampwork with small punches that resemble tools used in decorating leather goods. Silver applique and overlay and cut-out openwork are additional decorative techniques.

Indian jewelry usually is fashioned of silver. Other metals including gold, copper, brass, and nickel silver or German silver (an alloy of nickel, zinc, and copper with no precious metal content) occasionally may be used, instead. Silver of varying purity may be utilized, with "fine silver" (.999 pure), "sterling" silver (.925 silver and .075 copper), and "coin" silver (.900 silver and .100 copper) the most frequent choices. Only a small percentage of handmade jewelry articles made from silver are actually marked "sterling," ".925," or some other designation. A local jeweler can test a piece chemically with nitric acid, however, to verify the metal content. (A drop of nitric acid on an inconspicuous spot will turn sterling silver gray or nickel silver blueish.)

Closed-center wrought silver concha pin, ca. 1920's or 1930's. The concha form is one of the most widely recognized types of Southwestern Indian jewelry. The "concha," which is Spanish for "shell," is usually a round or oval disc of silver with a scalloped edge. It traditionally is embossed and stamped with a radiating central design and is often set with turquoise.

Quality of Workmanship

It is difficult at first to distinguish genuine hand-made from machine-made jewelry. Buyers always should carefully examine the edges and backs of jewelry pieces. Stress marks should be visible on the back of silver that has been hand wrought or hammered. Hand cast silver usually has a distinctive grainy texture to the reverse. If the workmanship is of good quality, jewelry cabochons, tabs, or beads of stone or shell should be even and well-polished and finished.

Better pieces of jewelry often are fashioned of thicker or heavier gauge silver. Edges of handmade pieces usually have traces of filemarks used to smooth the rough or sharp spots. Handmade silver beads generally have slightly irregular raised holes that have been punched from the inside out before soldering together the two hemispheres of the beads. Repetitive units of large jewelry pieces—such as squash blossom beads on a necklace or concha slides on a belt—should vary slightly from one another if they are completely handmade. Finally, some pieces that look handmade actually may have been assembled from individual pre-made parts obtained at trading posts or crafts shops.

By learning to examine carefully the stone, the metal, and the quality of workmanship of a piece of jewelry, a collector soon should be able to recognize a good quality piece of jewelry without being deceived.

Reverse of Navajo-style hand cast brooch (figure on page 84). The back of this hand cast piece is pitted with tiny holes which have been partly smoothed off by filing. The backs of machine-made or spin-cast examples can be distinguished from this traditional hand cast work by flow lines or streaky marks acquired during the spin cast cooling process.

Single strand of Navajo-style handmade silver beads. The timeless quality of these silver beads has ensured their continuing popularity since the late 1800's. These silver beads were made in two halves that were soldered together. The seam was then smoothed off and polished. The punched holes in the handmade beads were made prior to soldering. They poke outward from the spheres, which is probably the best clue to use for distinguishing a handmade from a machine-made bead. The portrait of a young Navajo girl wearing traditional jewelry, velveteen blouse, and full cotton skirt dates to the turn of the century.

The hallmark of the contemporary Santo Domingo ueblo silversmith Harold Lovato consists of initials plus a corn plant. This mark is cast into many of the two-sided handcast pieces for which he is well-known.

Documenting the Jewelry

Many articles of Indian jewelry bear the hallmark of the craftsman who created them. The maker's mark may consist of an engraved name, a cast initial or two, or a stamped symbol. When buying a piece of jewelry, a collector should ask the vendor to identify the maker if possible. If asked, the vendor often will write down this information on the receipt for the article. If a piece of jewelry bears a hallmark which is unknown to the vendor, the buyer might research the piece at a later date. Authors Barton and Margaret Wright and Mark Bahti, among others, have listed hallmarks of many native craftsmen. Tribal cooperatives and guilds also are often able to identify the maker of a marked piece of jewelry. Also, any other information about a piece of jewelry, such as the tribal origin, the probable age of the piece, or the mine the turquoise came from, should be recorded if known at the time of purchase.

Close comparison of these two pairs of butterfly spacers from concha belts reveals the difference between individual die stampwork (left) and unit stampwork (right). Although both sets of spacers are handmade, the left examples required more handiwork. Close visual comparison of the right examples shows that they are essentially identical. Visual comparison of the left examples reveals slight differences in spacing and placement of design elements as well as the lightly scribed guidelines of the craftsman.

Hallmarks of native American silversmiths, ca. 1970-1985. Although older jewelry is usually unsigned, some silversmiths occasionally began to use hallmarks on their jewelry after about 1930. Many contemporary smiths today sign the jewelry they create. Their identifying mark often consists of their name or initials. In some cases, particularly among the Hopi, a pictographic clan symbol is used. The double eagle feather mark (lower left) for example, is the hallmark of Hopi silversmith Vernon Mansfield who is a member of the Sun clan which uses eagle symbols.

Pawn Jewelry

In addition to newly made articles, older jewelry occasionally may be purchased. Some of the older jewelry that becomes available for sale is referred to as "pawn jewelry." Pawned items are material goods held by a trader as collateral for a loan of cash to their owner. If the owner does not repay the loan within an allotted period of time, the trader essentially "forecloses" on the loan and the pawned material—such as pawn jewelry—becomes "dead." The trader holds "dead pawn" for four months for the owner before the item becomes available for sale to dealers or the general public. On the average during a given year, only 5% to 7% of all pawned jewelry goes "dead"; the rest is reclaimed by its owners.

Contrary to popular belief, pawn jewelry is not always old, nor is it always handmade. (Occasionally, even non-Indian material may be found in pawn.) Pawn may include any item of monetary value that an Indian might give as security, ranging from Czechoslovakian crystal beads to a gold charm bracelet, a saddle, gun, or shawl. Though usually of Indian manufacture—many traders in the Southwest will not give cash loans for non-traditional items—pawn jewelry should be examined carefully and the history of the piece should be established. Pawn tickets that accompany many dead pawn items are no longer released to the buyer at the time of sale. Any information available on the ticket should be recorded by the buyer when purchasing an article.

Care of Jewelry

Indian jewelry, like any other type of accessory, occasionally may have to be cleaned or repaired. Often the store where a piece is purchased will have a resident silversmith or will know whom to contact about repairing an item. A few simple precautions and common sense care of the jewelry should prolong its life so that a visit to the repair shop will probably never be needed. Jewelry should be handled with care. Cuff bracelets and other pieces should not be bent because stones may pop out. The Indian jewelry is heavier than other types of costume jewelry and quality jewelry, and it is very easy to bang rings or clunk heavy najas when leaning forward.

Turquoise stones should be kept away from oil, detergents, and harsh cleaning agents which may alter the color and texture of the stone. Paste polishes and jewelry cleaning solutions also may affect the stones in Indian jewelry and should never be utilized. Instead, a polishing cloth with jeweler's rouge should be used to buff the silver. The jeweler's rouge cloth will remove tarnish from the surface without damaging stones and without polishing dark areas of the silver that the craftsman deliberately oxidized to heighten the contrast of the silver design.

A stone occasionally will come loose from its setting or a strand of beads will break. These broken items should be taken to a knowledgeable repair shop or jeweler. Some precautions may be taken to help prevent this type of breakage, though. Stones should be checked periodically. If they wiggle in their settings or if the bezels holding the stones seem loose, repair is needed. Some simple repairs can be made by the owner. A tiny amount of white glue such as the polyvinyl acetate (PVA) emulsion *Sobo®* carefully placed between the edge of a loosened stone and its mount will help to secure the stone. The edges of a silver bezel usually can be pressed in around the loosened stone to help tighten the setting, as well. Only an expert craftsman can properly replace a stone once it has been lost. Furthermore, because turquoise comes in many varieties, it is often difficult or impossible to match the replacement stone precisely with the original. So, inexpensive precautions like those mentioned above are advised.

The stringing of necklaces also should be examined regularly. Heavy beads put a lot of stress on the chain or string. Foxtail chain or multi-filament nylon are the most durable materials for stringing necklaces. Silver beads and squash blossoms should be strung on foxtail chain, while turquoise or shell heishi should be on multi-filament nylon. Cotton string, dental floss, plastic coated wire, monofilament materials, and even simple link chain may last only a short time before wearing out and breaking. Owners should examine stress points, such as sections near and around the clasp, for possible fraying, kinks, or other signs of potential breakage. Necklaces should be restrung immediately if any wear is visible or suspected. Some individuals automatically have a necklace professionally restrung on high quality material at the time of purchase, if the original material does not seem to be durable.

"Dead pawn" jewelry. Indian jewelry often is pawned by its owner as a way to raise immediate cash. Pawn tickets are no longer released with the jewelry at the time of a sale.

A view into the pawn vault at Tobe Turpen's Trading Company, Gallup, New Mexico. Pegboard provides a convenient way of sorting and storing quantities of Indian jewelry. Many trading posts, such as this company, serve as safe deposit vaults for the Indians. Some Indians will bring in $4,000-$5,000 worth of jewelry at one time and pawn it for $10.00, just to have the trader keep it safe for them.

Storage of Jewelry

Each piece of jewelry should be stored separately. Soft cotton handkerchiefs or silk scarfs or tissue may be used to wrap and pad jewelry. Clear ziplock bags or clear plastic boxes are useful for visibly storing pieces. Plastic should be of inert polyethylene; less stable plastics give off fumes that may tarnish or discolor the jewelry.

If all of these guidelines for buying and caring for Indian jewelry are followed, a collector should be able to build an interesting and satisfying collection of high quality, handmade Indian jewelry. In addition, owners will know how to care for their jewelry properly so that it will give them a lifetime of pleasure and enjoyment.

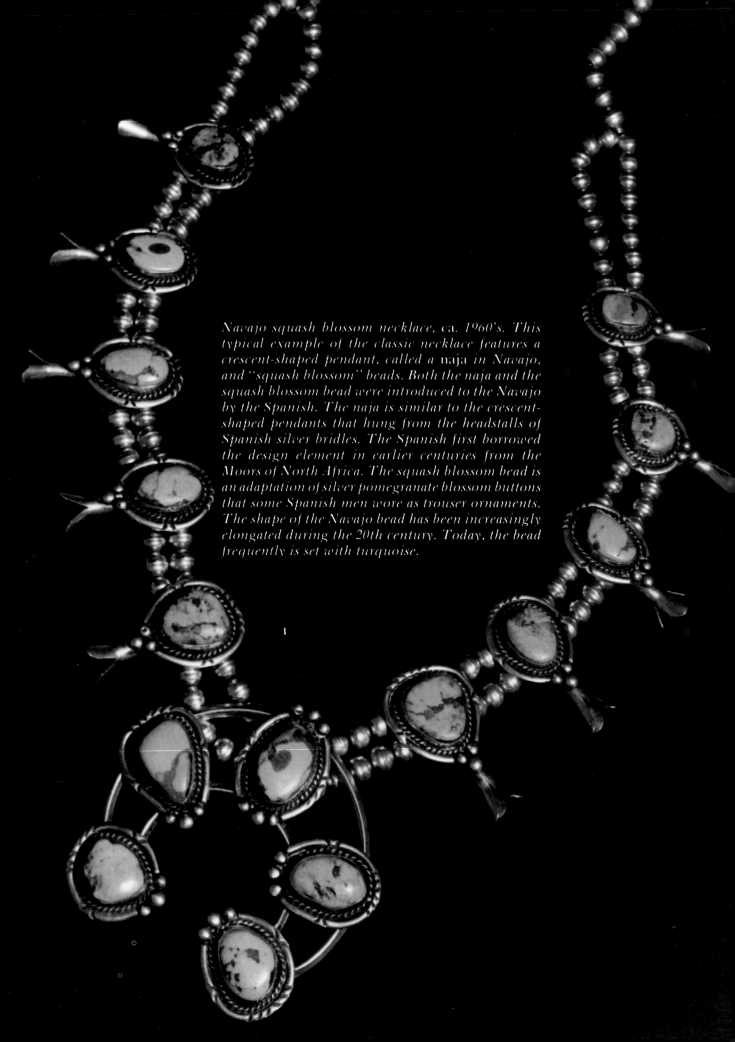

Navajo squash blossom necklace, ca. 1960's. This typical example of the classic necklace features a crescent-shaped pendant, called a *naja* in Navajo, and "squash blossom" beads. Both the naja and the squash blossom bead were introduced to the Navajo by the Spanish. The naja is similar to the crescent-shaped pendants that hung from the headstalls of Spanish silver bridles. The Spanish first borrowed the design element in earlier centuries from the Moors of North Africa. The squash blossom bead is an adaptation of silver pomegranate blossom buttons that some Spanish men wore as trouser ornaments. The shape of the Navajo bead has been increasingly elongated during the 20th century. Today, the bead frequently is set with turquoise.

Navajo

"Bluebird wore a beautiful robe of blue beads and on his head a bright blue cloud. In his right hand he held a rattle made of blue turquoise and in his left a stalk of blue corn. And when the people asked what he had brought, Bluebird said: 'I bring you blue sky, summer rain and soft corn.'"

—*From a Navajo myth*

The Navajo call themselves "Diné", which means "the people." Their Athapascan language is similar to those of the Apache groups of the Southwest and related to those of Athapascan peoples living in northwestern Canada. The ancestors of the Navajo were hunters and gatherers from the north who travelled in small bands and wandered into the Southwest perhaps 500 to 800 years ago. Both the agriculturally-oriented puebloans already living in the Southwest and, in later centuries, the Spanish conquistadores, missionaries, settlers, and traders who introduced sheep, goats, the modern-day horse, metal working and other novelties greatly influenced Navajo life.

Today, the Navajo grow some crops, and many raise sheep and other livestock, in addition to holding other sorts of jobs. Tribal revenues come from livestock, from uranium, coal, gas and oil leases, from timber sales, and from wages. The creation of turquoise and silver jewelry, colorful Navajo rugs, and other crafts adds to this income.

An octagonal-shaped Navajo hogan located in Canyon de Chelly, Arizona, early 1980's. The hogan is the traditional style of home for the Navajo, although many families today live in frame homes.

A Navajo woman and child pose in front of their hogan, early 20th century. The woman wears a velveteen blouse with turquoise jewelry including a tab necklace with joclas. The young girl enjoys a Hershey's chocolate bar, payment from the photographer for posing for the picture.

Navajo-style concha belt, ca. 1985. This recent example in silver and turquoise looks as traditional as one of the earliest Navajo concha belts made, illustrated in this painting of the subject by an anonymous artist inspired by R. C. Gorman's "Peshlakai's Concho." Notice that early conchas from the late 19th century, such as the painted example, often had openwork centers. Only in the 20th century did conchas with closed centers and turquoise sets become the preferred style. Today, both styles share their considerable popularity with more contemporary, innovative versions.

In 1846 the United States assumed control of the territory of New Mexico. Between the years of 1864 and 1868, Colonel Kit Carson and the military tried to subdue continuing Navajo raids by moving most of the Navajo to the Bosque Redondo reservation on the Pecos River near Fort Sumner, New Mexico. The relocation attempt proved disastrous economically and socially, so in 1868 the people were released and the population gradually recovered. Today, the Navajo live on huge reservations in northern Arizona and New Mexico and southeastern Utah. Their primary reservation surrounds the Hopi mesas in northeastern Arizona. The Navajo nation now numbers more than 160,000 people and is the nation's largest tribe.

Modern Navajo culture is a blend of the old and the new. Navajo homes, for example, range from contemporary frame houses to modernized versions of the round hogan to traditional earth-covered structures. Navajo women may wear blue jeans and flannel shirts, or permanent press blouses and polyester-blend slacks or skirts, or they may continue to dress more traditionally in the colorful velveteen blouses and full cotton skirts which have been standard since the late Victorian era. Whatever the preferred mode of dress, most Navajo garb is accessorized with turquoise and silver jewelry. Even young children usually wear small turquoise and silver bracelets, necklaces and earrings.

The blend of the traditional and the contemporary is apparent in Navajo jewelry. Navajo silversmiths always have emphasized bold, simple silver jewelry and have used turquoise, coral, or other materials as accents for the silver. Tools, techniques, styles, and stone preferences have varied through the decades, though.

The Navajo were the first Southwest Indians to learn silversmithing. In the early 1850s a Navajo who came to be known as Atsidi Sani, or "Old Smith," initially acquired the skill of iron-working, then learned the rudiments of working silver from a Mexican platero, or silversmith, named Juan Anea, and an American blacksmith, George Carter, who worked a forge near Washington Pass in the Chuska Mountains. Silverwork of the Mexican plateros, as well as of neighboring Spanish and Plains Indian peoples, greatly influenced Navajo work. American and Mexican silver coins as well as ingots were used to create the earliest silver jewelry. Atsidi Sani and other smiths had available only simple handmade tools for creating engraved, stamped, filed and chiselwork designs on silver. Yet, Atsidi Sani persisted in developing the skill. During the years of confinement at Bosque Redondo, Navajo men were given tools for blacksmithing. Atsidi Sani was among several Navajo blacksmiths who ran two forges on the reservation and helped teach the craft to other Navajos. A small amount of iron, copper, brass and silver jewelry appears to have been made during this period, as well.

After their release from Bosque Redondo, many Navajo continued to work as blacksmiths and some eventually began silverworking. All mid-19th century Navajo silver was hand hammered. American coins, Mexican pesos, or ingots were used at various periods until the 1920's when various thicknesses of sheet silver and wire were introduced. Today these materials are used most extensively, and few smiths still use handmade tools, preferring power equipment instead. Another pioneer in Navajo silverworking was Atsidi Chon, or "Ugly Smith." He probably was the first Navajo to create a horse bridle of silver (around 1870), and he also may have fashioned the first Navajo concha belt. In about 1872, Atsidi Chon taught the craft to the Zuni smith Lanyade, and in 1880 Atsidi Chon or an apprentice named Peshlakai Atsidi (or Slender-Maker-of-Silver) was the first to set a turquoise stone in a silver bezel.

A Navajo silversmith's concha stamp, ca. 1910-1925. This hand-wrought iron stamp set consists of a male punch and a female die which are used together with a sheet of silver to create an oval sunburst plate for a concha or "shell" form.

These two Navajo-style silver bracelets are traditional in design. The Navajo band (left) is hand cast and dates to the early 1980's. The carinated bangle (right) with a triangular cross-section has carefully stamped decoration. The latter example was made by a native silversmith working at Laguna Pueblo in the mid-1980's. Stylistically, both examples resemble those made much earlier in the century.

By 1880, the Navajo were casting silver in sandstone or tufa, as well as creating hand-hammered work. In hand casting by the "sand-cast" method, the native craftsman traditionally carves the design to be cast into a two-piece block of sandstone or volcanic tuff or tufa. The stones are then blackened with smoke to keep the molten silver from sticking to the mold. On average, no more than five or six casts may be made before the tufa block wears out. Today, about 90% of handcasting is done using a concrete and oil mold, which allows the silver-smith to make a greater number of castings before the mold is no longer usable. Inexpensive machine-made spincast versions of hand castings are also made today and should not be confused with the true handmade castwork.

Traditional-style mold of volcanic tuff or tufa carved by silversmith White Eagle, early 1970's. This mold was used for casting the silver for a ketoh or belt buckle. The double-curve design element is said to represent leaves of the corn plant. On average, no more than five or six castings may be made before this type of tufa block wears out.

This massive Navajo buckle, ca. 1950, was hand cast using more than 6½ ounces of silver! It was finished with chisel work and stamping.

Grouping of six Navajo cuff bracelets. Navajo artisan Jan Thomas created the elegant turquoise, coral, and silver floral applique bracelet (upper right). Other artists fashioned the remaining examples. The silverwork of the center front bracelet is cast. The remaining handwrought examples were created using sheet and wire silver with a variety of lapidary materials including a bear claw (lower right), turquoise, coral, mother-of-pearl, and black jet.

Navajo overlay "wedding basket design" jewelry, ca. 1970-1985. This design is made in various forms including bolo ties, rings, bracelets, pins, earrings, pendants, buttons, and squash blossom necklaces. Highly popular as a style for sale to tourist markets in the 1970's, this design recently has enjoyed renewed popularity in the mid-1980's. These examples were created by B. Paya. The bolo tie with basket slide and miniatures on the tips was found in pawn jewelry. New pieces by the same artist are virtually identical. Copper has been combined with the silver overlay to create the characteristic red band found in all Navajo wedding baskets.

Navajo chip inlay bracelet, ca. 1960's-1970's. This heavy silver cuff bracelet of Navajo workmanship features good quality chip inlay of turquoise and coral. Chip inlay is a modern adaptation of two earlier techniques—mosaic inlay lapidary and overlay silverwork. Background areas of silver overlay that would be left black in the original overlay method are instead filled with an epoxy and fragments of turquoise, coral, black jet, or other material. Chip inlay work was first made in the early 1960's by Navajo smiths including Dean Kirk, Tom Singer, and other Singer family members.

Navajo craftsman Fannie Platero created this attractive pendant in the 1980's. Sterling silver sets off the exquisite green turquoise from Manassa, Colorado. The silver link chain is hand-wrought.

Navajo silver applique collar by Richard Thomas, early 1980's. A bear claw, turquoise, and coral are combined with intricate silver applique to create this impressive necklace resting against a bear skull.

Until the late 1890's, the Navajo made both hand hammered and hand cast silver jewelry mainly for themselves or for other Indians. From about 1900 on, though, they have created jewelry for commercial consumption also. At times, styles have become more standardized and have changed somewhat due to non-native influences. Indian traders and trading posts, tourists and railroads and, more recently, Americana buffs and high fashion enthusiasts have sought out native American jewelry that encapsulates the Navajo and life in the Old West. Navajo silversmiths have adapted their craft throughout the decades to accommodate changing tastes, as well as to meet their own demands. Yet, the popularity of the traditional hand wrought and cast silverwork has persisted. It may be decorated with silver applique, embossing, die stamping, file work or chisel-work and may be accented with turquoise or other stones, all of which have been used throughout the past century. The Navajo recently have begun to borrow methods from other tribes, including silver overlay, and mosaic stone inlay and stone channelwork, which they use alone or in combination with techniques that are recognized as more typically Navajo. However, pieces that incorporate these borrowed methods still have a characteristic Navajo look or feel to them.

...uttons, or *"Yoo nil chini,"* ...n Navajo. *A wad cutter (left)* ...s used to cut out a button ...lank of silver (lower left). ...hen, the blank is embossed ...ith one or more dies (right) ...f the silversmith's choosing. ...lany stamped design varieties ...re made in this way. The ...utton at the lower right has ...een made into an earring, or ...Jaatl ool" in Navajo. Fos-...ilized fish are found in several ...reas of the American West.

...wo Navajo turquoise and silver rings, probably ...970's. The Navajo frequently wear silver jewelry ...at is set either with clusters of small stonework or ...ith more massive single stones. Navajo craftsmen ...ade both of these rings, although the petitpoint ...uster work technique (left) by Navajo smith James ...lason is more usually associated with Zuni artisans.

Three Navajo-style pins show the range of traditional silverworking techniques that Navajo silversmiths use. The methods include a hand wrought, embossed, and stamped oval concha brooch (top), an applique silver and turquoise pin/pendant (left), and a hand cast pin with a turquoise set (right).

Dress ornaments. Frontal detail of button-like dress ornaments on the Navajo velveteen blouse.

The traditional dress of Navajo women since late Victorian times has consisted of a velveteen blouse and long, gathered cotton skirt. This hand-sewn blouse of red velveteen dates to about 1940. It is liberally decorated with more than 275 buttons and dress ornaments. Some of the domed buttons are earlier, probably dating to about 1900. This blouse originally belonged to a member of the Begay family living on the Navajo Reservation near Cameron, Arizona.

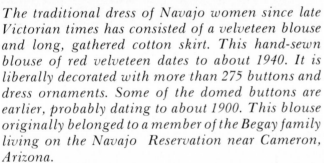

Buttons. Shoulder and collar detail of a variety of buttons sewn onto the Navajo velveteen blouse. These include plain domed buttons, several types of domed and fluted "hogan" buttons, flat Liberty head dime buttons, and "butterfly" shaped buttons. The flat buttons probably post-date 1940 while the domed buttons are earlier. Traders encouraged Indians to adopt the flat style of button making so that buttons would be more salable to the tourist market. Flat buttons were more easily sewn to garments than were the earlier domed buttons that the Indians so loved to make and wear.

Buttons. Detail of silver buttons outlining the yoke of the Navajo velveteen blouse. The buttons not only are attractive ornaments to look at but also are pleasing to listen to. They jingle musically when the wearer of the blouse moves about.

The squash blossom necklace and the concha belt are considered the most typical forms of Navajo silversmithing, although both are made by other peoples as well. They have been created in many variations during the past century. Other forms typical of the Navajo and made since the mid-1800's are still regularly worn and used today by Navajos and non-Indians alike. These include silver buttons, bracelets, rings, earrings, manta pins, and silver horse bridles. Fewer forms include hair combs and barrettes, tie tacks, money clips, cuff links, watch bands, bolo ties, and key chains. All may be made in traditional coin or sterling silver and turquoise.

Or they may be fashioned from other metals including nickel silver (which has no precious metal content), gold, or other metals. In addition to turquoise or coral, a variety of colorful materials is used today to accent the silverwork. While some of these materials are locally available, others are imported: ivory, ironwood, black obsidian, onyx, sodalite, azurite, lapis lazuli, chrysocolla, malachite, and various types of shell such as abalone, yellow freshwater clam, pink freshwater mussel, and pen shell. Precious stones are occasionally mounted alone or combined with gem quality turquoise in gold settings made by Navajo artists.

This contemporary Zuni pendant with handmade link chain portrays the Sun God kachina. The combination of lapidary techniques—including mosaic inlay, petitpoint, and needlepoint—is unusual to find in a single piece of jewelry. Benjamin Zuni, Jr., created this action kachina in 1979 using blue turquoise, black jet, red coral, white mother-of-pearl, and sterling silver. It is #5 in a limited edition of ten.

Zuni

"As the Ant People were preparing to take their bundles of dry earth and grass seeds to the upper world, First Woman told them to take bits of the hard blue stone of the sky so there would also be some hard rock in the new world. So when the Ant People went through the sky tunnel, they bit off pieces of the blue rock and carried them to the surface of the muddy island. And so it is that we can still find beautiful blue turquoise."

—From a Zuni myth

The Zuni, or A'shiwi (which means "the flesh"), make their home today in western New Mexico. They are the modern-day descendants of several different cultural groups including remnants of the ancient Mogollon and Anasazi peoples. The Zuni speak a Penutian language all their own, called Zunian, and their population presently numbers about 6,000 individuals. Although the Zuni farm and raise livestock, jewelry making contributes substantially to their cash income. Some Zuni pottery is still made for commercial sale, but weaving and basket making are almost forgotten arts among the Zuni today.

Many Zuni families live in the old village built on the site of Halona, one of the fabled "Seven Cities of Cibola" sought by the Spanish explorer Coronado. Even today, the pueblo looks similar to the mid-19th century view of it, shown here below. Many Zuni women still bake native bread outdoors in sand-colored adobe hornos, or ovens. Twisted firewood stacked in bundles beside these loaf-shaped ovens adds to the color of the picturesque old pueblo. Traditional religious ceremonies and dances are still observed at Zuni. Some, such as the impressive Shalako Dance performed in late November or early December and colorful kachina dances of the spring and summer months, are open to visitors.

This matching Zuni-style cluster bracelet and ring were made by B. Natewa in the early 1980's. They set off an early view of Zuni Pueblo, made in the 1850's by artist H.B. Mollhausen.

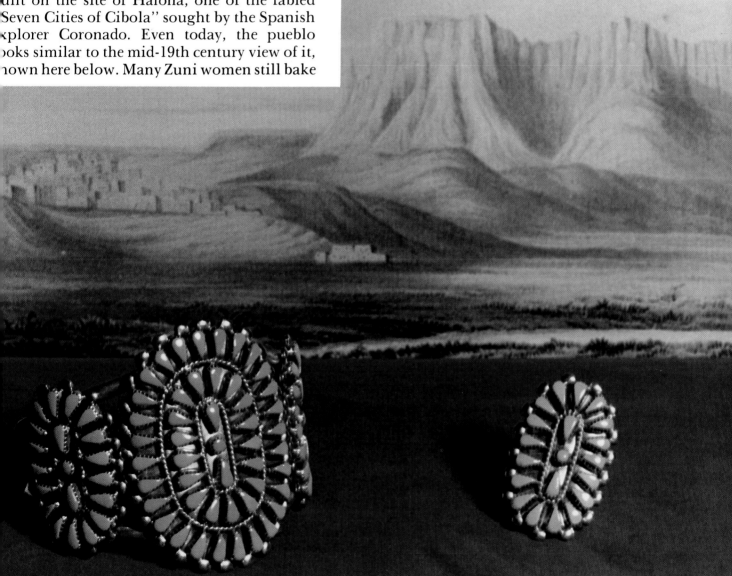

In earlier centuries, the Zuni lived in seven villages in the Zuni Valley. The biggest of these pueblos was Hawikuh, inhabited from about 1380 A.D. to 1670 A.D. It was another of the "Seven Cities" which the Spanish thought held the elusive treasure of the New World. This pueblo survived 16th century Spanish contact, but the Zuni abandoned it due to increasing pressures from Apache and Navajo peoples. The archaeologist F. W. Hodge excavated the ruins between 1917 and 1923. Pieces of turquoise jewelry—including some fetishes and examples of mosaic work—were recovered during these excavations and lend great time-depth to the Zuni tradition of working with turquoise and shell. Since their discovery, these artifacts also have inspired modern-day Zuni artisans to reach back into their past and revive traditional turquoise stonework.

Metalworking has had a different history among the Zuni. In about 1830, the Zuni learned to work with copper and brass salvaged from old kettles. Not until some four decades later, though, did they begin silvercrafting. In about 1872, the Navajo smith Atsidi Chon, who traded frequently with the Zuni for livestock, taught a Zuni man named Lanyade the skill of silversmithing. Much of the earliest silver jewelry of the Zuni is essentially identical to the Navajo work which spawned it. Forms, settings, and designs are all very similar.

The early Zuni pieces were of plain, handwrought silver and were occasionally decorated with simple techniques such as die-stamping or rocker engraving. Around 1890 they began to include turquoise also, as had their Navajo neighbors. A smith named Keneshde is credited with being the first Zuni to set turquoise from the Cerrillos mines near Santa Fe in silver, and it is said that he taught himself to do so without ever having seen any jewelry set with stones. Until about 1920, the Zuni fashioned jewelry primarily for themselves and other native peoples. But by about 1930, the Zuni were creating much of their jewelry for tourists. By ten years later, jewelry making had become a major means of earning revenue.

The emphasis on turquoise small stone work, which today is most strongly associated with the modern Zuni jewelry making tradition, began to emerge in jewelry made in the 1920's. The distinctive lapidary work developed partly from a revival of prehistoric jewelry making styles discovered during excavation of Hawikuh. Its popularity in modern commercial markets also has helped to foster the technique. Clusterwork, which groups together many individual stones in a setting of individual silver bezels, first appeared in about 1920. This technique was followed by petitpoint cluster lapidary which uses round, oval, or teardrop shaped stones. In about 1940 the needlepoint style appeared, incorporating long, narrow stones that are pointed at both ends.

Zuni petitpoint necklace and earrings, derivative squash blossom style, ca. 1950. Careful silverwork, small stonework, and hand soldered silver beads give this set an especially dainty look. Matching earrings were made from two petitpoint beads that originally were a seventh pair on the necklace.

Zuni-style cluster pin with unusual openwork and embossed lunettes of silver. This pin is made in the manner of Roman Ramoncito; a very similar example by him won a prize at the 1958 Gallup Ceremonial. The former owner of this "dead pawn" brooch lived at Taos Pueblo and probably traded with the Zuni for this brooch.

The carving of small fetish-like animals, birds, and other life forms in turquoise, shell, coral, jet, and other materials to be used in jewelry began in the 1920's and was inspired by similar ancient examples found at Hawikuh. The master fetish carver Leekya Desyee was among the workmen who discovered the prehistoric stone carvings. Other carvers who adopted this style as early as the 1930's include Lee Edaakie, Dishta, and David and Mary Tsikewa. Mosaic inlay and overlay was also found on some artifacts excavated at Hawikuh, and in 1935 Zuni silversmith Teddy Weake revived the method in his work. An outgrowth

The Zuni love to wear massive turquoise necklaces. This beautiful example of rolled turquoise beads includes three large carved turquoise leaves, each of which is about three inches long. This necklace was fashioned probably ca. 1970, although the Zuni have carved similar turquoise leaf forms for decades.

Zuni butterfly inlay jewelry, 1960's-1970's. For decades, the butterfly has been the most popular life form that the Zuni have created in jewelry. Here, a necklace, belt buckle, ring, bracelet, and earrings seem to hover on the page! The original owner of this treasured set collected one piece at a time. Most of the silverwork was done by Mary Livingston Benally. The mosaic inlay lapidary was created by several Zuni craftsmen, among them Juan Oshki.

Necklaces of fetish-like animals and birds have been made in the Southwest since prehistoric times. Modern examples were first made in the 1920's, after ancient carved fetishes were excavated at the Zuni Pueblo site of Hawikuh. The necklaces illustrated here date to the late 1970's and early 1980's and are very popular today. A fetish is a special natural or carved rock in which a spirit is thought to dwell. If the fetish is treated well, it will supernaturally assist its owner. The Zuni fetish bowl illustrated here is made for commercial sale to tourists and collectors. Edna Leki, grand-daughter of famous Zuni fetish carver Leekya Desyee, and two of her daughters carved the animal fetishes for this fetish bowl, ca. 1980. Edna gets her pots from Acoma. Then, she attaches the fetishes with aged leather strips. Eight fetishes encircle this bowl, and four more live inside on an offering of specially prepared blue cornmeal.

of this style called channel inlay, which sets stones into individual sunken silver frames so that they are flush with the level of the silver, was being made by 1940. Until the 1950's, many of the silver frames for channel work were being fashioned by Navajo silversmiths and traded to the Zuni. Domed channel inlay, which encrusts the silver frames with carefully rounded turquoise insets, is a more recent variety of channel work. It has been popular despite being quite fragile because the highly-domed turquoise is not protected by the silver setting.

All of the techniques utilizing small worked stones are drawn from traditional roots in the early Zuni culture. The market economy of the 20th century has nurtured the revival and development of the beautiful lapidary work along traditional avenues. The same commercial environment also has helped to shape contemporary jewelry making and to open new directions, based on changing preferences of buyers as well as on changing approaches of the Zuni artisans themselves. Today, the Zuni Craftsman Cooperative plays an important role in helping to market these beautiful creations in stone and silver and in guiding individual craftsmen in traditional and new directions.

Opposite page:

Zuni collar with mosaic inlay lapidary, ca. 1985. Alex and Marylita Boone of Zuni, New Mexico, created this elegant necklace with matching earrings. They used silver, turquoise, red coral, black jet, and yellow freshwater clamshell.

These three Zuni-style bracelets were created using different lapidary techniques. Dave and Celia Nizto teamed up to fashion the silver applique and turquoise "needlepoint" bangle (left), while H. Morgan made the fish-scale "channel inlay" bracelet (center) for Tobe Turpen's Trading Company in Gallup. The bangle on the right is encrusted with "domed channel inlay" work in carefully shaped turquoise.

Zuni style necklace of channel inlay, early 1980's. J.D. Massif used turquoise, coral, dark penshell, and yellow clamshell mosaic segments to create this popular version of the Sunface kachina. The collar rests against an ancient Southwestern petroglyph of concentric circles, symbolizing the sun itself.

Hopi

"Turquoise, for Indians of the Southwest, is a legendary stone; it represents the sky... to look upon (the Sky Stone) in the morning was to bring success for the rest of the day; it brought good health and happiness; it represented the heroes and the deeds and the settings of the creation myths. It was a gift from the gods—and a gift to the gods."

—*Carl Rosnek, in* Skystone and Silver

The Hopi, or "Peaceful Ones," trace much of their ancestry back to the Anasazi, "Enemy Ancestors," who were prehistoric inhabitants of the Four Corners region. The Hopi speak a Shoshonean language, and the Hopi nation currently numbers about 8,500 members. The Hopi reservation is surrounded by the Navajo reservation and is located in northeastern Arizona. Most of the modern-day Hopi live in a dozen separate villages. Many of the pueblos are located near or on the terraces of three high, flat mesas that project southwestward from a larger formation called Black Mesa. The sand-colored pueblos were built using stone from the mesa cliffs, and they easily blend into the arid desert landscape surrounding them. One of the pueblos called Old Oraibi, on the westernmost Third Mesa, was built before 1150 A.D. and is said to be the oldest continuously occupied village in the United States. Small natural springs at the foot of the mesas help to nurture the gardens of this primarily agricultural people. Only one Hopi village, Moenkopi, irrigates its fields; the remaining pueblos rely entirely on the springs and scanty rainfall for success of their crops. Many of the Hopi ceremonial dances—which usually are open to the public—are performed as prayers for rain and good harvests.

The Hopi Pueblo of Walpi on First Mesa. Today, stone buildings of this pueblo look the same as when A.C. Vroman photographed this view in 1897.

Opposite page:
Five Hopi overlay bracelets, 1980's. Early Morning Singer or Dawn Kachina, named Talavai, pauses over a selection of Hopi overlay bracelets by several different artisans. Fret motifs on prehistoric pottery inspired designs on these modern versions which exhibit some of the endless variations of the fret design.

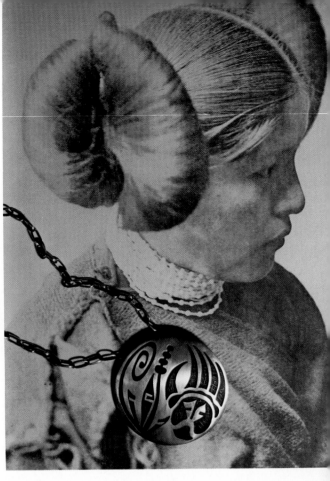

Hopi overlay earrings, ca. 1970's, and vintage postcards, ca. 1900. Hopi country has been a popular destination for travelers since the days of the Old West. Only the souvenirs have changed. Here, two Hopi women are dressed in traditional garb and jewelry. Their different hairstyles indicate the married status of the mother (left) and unmarried status of her daughter (right).

Hopi fields in Arizona. Side-hill fields on the Hopi Reservation near Oraibi are planted with various crops including rows of corn, beans, and melons.

Hopi silver overlay pin/pendant and handmade chain, ca. 1980. This stylized representation of the badger paw is a popular design element in Southwestern Indian jewelry.

The Hopi still observe many of their traditional activities, in spite of cultural pressures from neighboring Indian peoples as well as from Spanish-Colonial and Anglo-American peoples over the past 450 years. In addition to farming and working for wages at a variety of jobs, the Hopi earn cash income from native arts and crafts. Their pottery, wood-carvings, weaving, and basketry have strong, often unbroken, roots in the past. Some—such as the twill-plaited ring basket used for winnowing—have been created in traditional styles that have changed only slightly through many centuries. Hopi silverwork is of considerably more recent vintage than most of the other native crafts, since it was first adopted only about 100 years ago. Yet, contemporary Hopi silversmiths draw their designs and much of their inspiration from Hopi prehistory and early history.

Early Hopi jewelry was made from natural materials including turquoise, shell, wood, and seeds. Silverworking was introduced to the Hopi in about 1890. After learning silversmithing from the Navajo Atsidi Chon in 1872, the Zuni smith Lanyade began to trade some of his own silver jewelry creations among the Hopi, apparently in return for handwoven native cotton textiles. Later, in about 1890, Lanyade taught his craft to a Hopi named Sikyatala or "Yellow Light." Early handwrought silver beads, rings, and bracelets made by the Hopi are virtually indistinguishable from those made by Zuni and Navajo smiths. Some Hopi created cast silverwork, as well. Not until the 1930's did a distinctive Hopi tribal style begin to emerge, and it developed only with non-native encouragement. This style is known as *overlay* and is today the most widely recognized type of Hopi Indian silverwork.

Hopi overlay jewelry. The silver collar and clip earrings have designs that are taken from nature, as well as from prehistoric and historic native pottery, basketry and textiles. A colorful Hopi wicker tray and a coiled kachina plaque serve as the backdrop for these elegant examples of this jewelry style.

Pinyon pine nuts, a popular native Southwestern food, accent these examples of Hopi overlay jewelry. The pin by Vernon Mansfield sports an antelope, while the reversible double-overlay pendant depicts the Pima Siuhu Ki "man in the maze" design (obverse) and footprint and maze (reverse).

Hopi silver overlay pendant. This stylized eagle is the creation of Victor Coochwytewa, who began silversmithing in 1940. He was among the earliest group of Hopi craftsmen to make jewelry in the overlay style. The dotted stippling and lined chiselwork decoration are ornamental additions not usually seen on most overlay work.

Hopi silver overlay as a distinctive technique began in 1938 through a project which Dr. Harold Colton and his wife Mary Russell Colton of the Museum of Northern Arizona initiated. Native participants were encouraged to create a unique type of jewelry that would be recognized as Hopi. Overlay using designs drawn from traditional pottery, textile, and basketry sources resulted. After World War II ended, the G.I. Bill paid for Hopi veterans to take classes in silversmithing, and overlay became the established Hopi style of jewelry. The Hopi Silvercraft Guild, founded in 1949, provides both a workshop and a commercial outlet for silversmiths, thus encouraging and supporting their artistic development.

In overlay, two sheets of silver are soldered together after cutting out designs in the top layer so that the under layer is visible. The under layer is blackened or oxidized, and the Hopi smiths usually texture it with chisel marks or stamp-work. Some Navajo and Rio Grande puebloan smiths also create silver overlay, but they generally use a plain, untextured black under-layer. Hopi silversmiths often buff their finished jewelry pieces with steel wool which gives the silver a matte or satin finish. The mechanized technique of spin-casting recently has been used to mass-produce less expensive imitations of Hopi silver overlay. Buyers should take care to distinguish the real, handmade overlay from machine-made look-alikes.

Turquoise, red coral, and other materials occasionally have been set in Hopi overlay jewelry. For the most part, though, the elegant silver overlay has stood alone. Today, some contemporary Hopi artisans—under the leadership of pioneering artists Charles Loloma and Preston Monongye, among others—are fashioning inlay and cast silver jewelry and working in gold. As these artists break away from recent cultural restraints, they are reaching back into early native traditions for inspiration. As they combine fresh approaches with overlay and other contemporary influences, they are creating new dimensions in Hopi silversmithing.

This silver Hopi overlay collar is exceptionally well crafted. It is an early example of the work of the master craftsman Preston Monongye. Several unusual features give this necklace an especially sensual attractiveness, including the complexly wrought chain, the polished finish, the highly domed overlay plates, and the superior texturing of the matte black background. Many of Monongye's more recent pieces combine different techniques and materials in a style that goes beyond traditional Hopi silversmithing bounds.

Hopi silver overlay earrings, ca. 1985. The Hopi Arts and Crafts Silvercraft Cooperative Guild began in 1949. Today, it is located at Second Mesa. The guild is a mecca for visitors and serves as a major outlet for jewelry and other arts which Hopi artisans create.

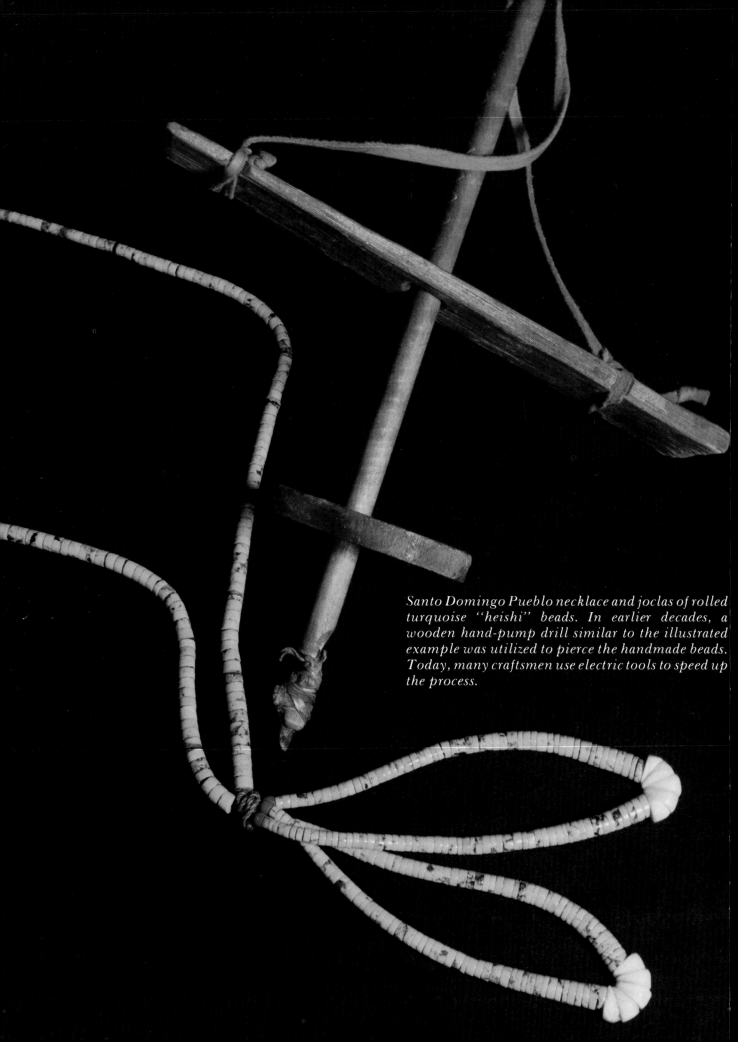

Santo Domingo Pueblo necklace and joclas of rolled turquoise "heishi" beads. In earlier decades, a wooden hand-pump drill similar to the illustrated example was utilized to pierce the handmade beads. Today, many craftsmen use electric tools to speed up the process.

Rio Grande Puebloans

"A little mud forge, a hammer, a simple punch, a three-cornered file, a stone or bit of iron for an anvil, a little clay for a crucible and some solder and brains—and there is your aboriginal smith."

—*Acoma silversmith, as described by Charles Lummis, 1896.*

The modern-day puebloans are descended predominantly from prehistoric Anasazi stock. They moved into the Rio Grande valley in the 14th century A.D., during a period of warfare and prolonged drought. Today, there are 18 Rio Grande pueblo reservations, in addition to Zuni and Hopi. These pueblos are: Acoma, Cochiti, Isleta, Jemez, Laguna, Nambe, Picuris, Pojoaque, San Felipe, San Ildefonso, San Juan, Sandia, Santa Ana, Santa Clara, Santo Domingo, Taos, Tesuque, and Zia. Although the pueblos of Acoma and Laguna are located to the west of the river valley, they generally are included in considerations of the Rio Grande pueblos. Altogether, the population of these pueblos totals about 30,000 people. Laguna is the largest and Picuris and Pojoaque the smallest, in terms of number of residents.

Taos Pueblo, New Mexico, produces a small amount of overlay jewelry today.

The picturesque Laguna Pueblo is the largest of the Rio Grande pueblos.

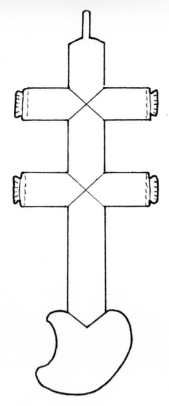

The double-barred cross has long been popular in the Rio Grande pueblos, probably because it resembles a dragonfly, an important and ancient water symbol in native life. This typical example from San Juan Pueblo in the 1890's probably was made at Laguna or Isleta and traded to a resident of San Juan.

Zuni (left) and Cochiti Pueblo (right) necklaces, early 1980's. Both of these necklaces of fetish-like animals and birds are strung on fine strands of brown olive shell heishi made at Santo Domingo Pueblo (left) and Cochiti Pueblo (right). The tiny bears, badgers, foxes, wolves, and mountain lions on the left example were made and strung by Zuni carver Lena Boone. Manuelita Flower of Cochiti Pueblo fashioned the miniature birds on the right. Zuni carvers usually add slightly more detail to their birds (see the earrings on page 88) than do Rio Grande puebloans.

Many of the Rio Grande pueblos began silver-working in the late 19th century, at about the same time as the Navajo, Zuni, and Hopi began to work the metal. Yet, few have continued to develop the skill to the same extent. Silver-smithing was learned at Acoma, Laguna, and Isleta in the 1870's and was practiced into the 20th century. Most jewelry was of plain silver, although one smith at Laguna, named Diego Ramos, originally from Isleta, began setting turquoise in silver after about 1910. Necklaces of hollow silver beads with double-barred crosses—called the Lorraine or Caravaca cross—were a specialty of Laguna and Isleta and were particularly popular among native Americans because the crosses resembled the dragonfly, an ancient water symbol.

Cochiti Pueblo has produced some silver and turquoise jewelry since the early 20th century. Most of this jewelry is bold and simple and was modelled on traditional Navajo work. Joseph

This Pueblo Indian employs traditional tools and techniques to produce rolled turquoise beads very similar to those that were popular with prehistoric cultures in the American Southwest.

nd Jerry Quintana are among the most widely
nown of the Cochiti silversmiths. The pueblo
orks primarily with shell and turquoise.
oday, the Flower family of Cochiti produces
ne shell "heishi" beadwork and carved bird
tishes that rival the better known Santo
omingo products. A small amount of silver
welry also has been made from time to time at
ther pueblos such as San Ildefonso, Taos, and
icuris. Most pueblo smiths have held a different
rimary job and have practiced silversmithing
s a second job or hobby. Generally, though,
ney have bartered with Navajo or Santo
omingo peddlers for the silver jewelry they
esired. Silver and turquoise jewelry more
ommonly has been made by peoples located to
ie west of the Rio Grande valley—the Navajo,
uni, Hopi, and even Laguna and Isleta. When
ie pueblos situated directly on the Rio Grande
ave made jewelry, they more typically have
orked with turquoise, stone and shell.

Santo Domingo Pueblo, like Cochiti, has
eated both silver and shell and turquoise
welry. Although the Santo Domingos traded
ith the Navajos for much of their silver jewelry,
ome did practice the craft. In 1893, Ralph
tencio became the first to learn the skill at
nto Domingo. Others were to follow. Old
nto Domingo silverwork resembles Navajo
welry. In the early 20th century, though, a style
stinctive to Santo Domingo developed which
lapted naturalistic bird and flower designs
om Santo Domingo pottery to silverworking.
 the early 1940's, some Santo Domingos began
 create these designs in silver overlay also. The
ork of Vidal Aragon (shown above) is an
kample of Santo Domingo overlay.

Santo Domingo Pueblo "storyteller" ring, overlay technique, ca. 1970's. The reflected image of a woman from Taos Pueblo floats behind this sterling silver overlay ring made by Vidal Aragon. The Santo Domingo silversmith is well-known for his fine overlay silverwork, which he began making in the 1940's. This "storyteller" ring depicts a seasonal theme that includes figures of deer, trees, and a mountain lion.

The inhabitants of many of the Rio Grande pueblos— and particularly Santo Domingo Pueblo—have made turquoise and shell beads for generations. Today, the Rio Grande puebloans are considered to be the finest bead makers. They often trade their beads to other peoples including the Zuni, Navajo, and Hopi. These examples were made at Santo Domingo Pueblo, except for the two-strand necklace (third from left) which the Flower family of Cochiti Pueblo made.

Santo Domingo traditionally has made rolled turquoise and shell "heishi" beads. The Rosetta family is especially well-known for their unusually fine hand-made beads. Most of the turquoise used in beadwork traditionally has come from the Cerrillos mines which are located near the Pueblo and are claimed as Santo Domingo property. Today, many different turquoises—even reconstituted turquoise—are used as well. Shell for beads traditionally has come from the Gulf of California and Pacific Ocean since prehistoric times. Olivella, spiny oyster, clam, abalone, and conus are among favorite exotic shell types used in Santo Domingo beadwork. To make a strand of beads, turquoise or shell fragments are drilled. Then they are strung on string or wire and carefully ground and polished into shape by pulling them across a grinding stone. Wooden hand worked pump drills used for drilling beads have been replaced more recently with power drills. Also, some beadmakers use electric grinding stones to speed the process of shaping the beads. The finer the strand of beads, the more expensive it usually will be. Most beads used and sold throughout the Southwest today are made at Santo Domingo. They may be traded to other tribes or sold to Indian arts dealers. Santo Domingos themselves peddle these beads widely, often bartering them for Navajo rugs, livestock, and silver, or selling them to merchants in Santa Fe, Albuquerque, or Gallup. Both bead making and silver working produce a considerable cash income for Santo Domingos today.

Two-strand necklace with joclas. The jocla necklace with turquoise tabs and shell and turquoise heishi is very popular among the tribes of the American Southwest. Though made by Rio Grande puebloans, it was regularly traded to and worn by other groups in the region. This example accents a view of a Navajo woman who is wearing typical clothing and jewelry.

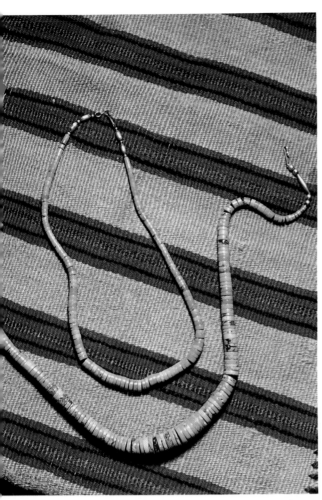

These rolled turquoise beads, or heishi, were made by Santo Domingo Pueblo Indians in the early 1980's. Similar strands may be purchased from craftsmen at the pueblo or from native vendors and shops in other locations.

Opposite page:
This four-strand necklace of clam shell heishi and red Mediterranean coral beads with "squaw wrap" finish has a timeless look to it. The traditional style has been worn in the Southwest for generations, yet its natural simplicity makes it popular in the world of high fashion as well. Saks Fifth Avenue of Phoenix has featured classic multistrand heishi and jocla necklaces similar to this example in its authentic Southwest Indian collection since the 1970's. Hopi piki bread of blue cornmeal supports this necklace.

Two very large green and blue turquoise nugget necklaces, early 1970's. The two colors of turquoise probably were mined at different locations in the Southwest.

Contemporary Navajo-style necklace, ca. 1985. T
leaf motif is especially popular among non-India
and always has sold well. Navajo silversmith Hostee
Goodluck was creating it for commercial sale by t
1920's. Here, the traditional and popular desi
element is interpreted in a new way.

New Directions in Indian Jewelry

"Our objectives are to experiment and test new ideas and techniques in art by using traditional Hopi designs and concepts as well as our own concepts of the inner Hopi."
— Fred Kabotie, Hopi Indian artist, 1977

Since the late 1960's and early 1970's, the established tribal or regional jewelry styles have been moving in new directions. Traditional techniques, forms, and designs are being combined with contemporary materials and innovations to create Indian jewelry that is more highly individualistic. Two Hopi artisans, Preston Monongye and Charles Loloma, were among the first native silversmiths to venture beyond the established boundaries of their traditional tribal styles. Their original creations are highly successful. They have been accepted by and also have served as inspiration for non-native and native markets and silversmiths. The jewelry of Monongye and Loloma—as well as creations of many other contemporary native artists—is acknowledged today in high fashion circles as "art by Indian artists" rather than simply as "Indian art."

This "new Indian" jewelry—a term coined by Monongye in a June 1972 article in *Arizona Highways*—draws on native cultural heritage and jewelry-making traditions for inspiration but is not constrained by the established limits. New materials such as gold, diamonds, rubies, malachite, lapis lazuli, and other precious and semiprecious stones and shell types (including paua or blue abalone from the South Pacific) have been added to the artists' range of acceptable choices. Sophisticated power tools enable craftsmen both to work with silver and to shape

This contemporary jewelry in 14K gold incorporates high-grade turquoise and other materials. It was styled by Carl Clark, ca. 1985, who is a Navajo artisan of the Manygoats clan. (Photo by Bill McLemore, courtesy of Gilbert Ortega Galleries of Fine Indian Arts.)

Santo Domingo Pueblo craftsman Harold Lovato created this contemporary cast pendant. He is well-known for his two-sided castwork, of which this pendant is an example. Its reverse (see page 36) bears his cast hallmark. Many of his pieces feature a more complex design on the reverse, as well.

stones for inlay in more intricate ways than were possible in the past. Design inspirations are drawn from 20th century life, as well as from the cultural background of more traditional Indian lifeways. Zuni inlay jewelry, for example, may depict Mickey Mouse or emblems from the Olympics as readily as kachinas or life forms native to the Southwest. Some Hopi silversmiths now create sandcast jewelry more frequently than overlay pieces. Similarly, Navajo artisans may fashion cluster or inlay jewelry and silver overlay, techniques that formerly were associated only with the Zuni and Hopi, respectively.

Much, but not all, contemporary jewelry is

This contemporary cuff bracelet combines traditional design elements in fine silver overlay work, giving the bracelet a lacy and delicate look not found in earlier examples. Sophisticated modern tools and materials have increased the options available to contemporary native silversmiths.

increasingly pan-Indian in manufacture, if not also in design. Some Zuni fetish necklaces, for example, may include fetishes carved by several members of a family. These fetishes may be strung on fine shell heishi beads that were made by Santo Domingo Pueblo people and traded to the Zuni. Similarly, some Navajo silversmiths may specialize in fashioning the silver mountings for jewelry, while other Navajo or Zuni craftsmen prepare lapidary for mounting in the silver.

As Indian jewelry moves in a greater variety of directions than existed earlier in this century, some native silversmiths are finding their own place in the mainstream of art. As in many other professions, some achieve this recognition due to their own skill and creativity. Others are now receiving the extra advantage of formal training through special courses and schools that promote the continuation of native arts. The Institute of American Indian Art in Santa Fe is among the most notable of these institutions. It encourages promising young native artists to develop technical proficiency while seeking individual ways of expressing their traditional heritage in artistic terms. While the creations of all artists at the school blend the ancient with the contemporary, some of their products look traditionally "Indian" while others are more cosmopolitan in overall effect. Neither extreme is either better or more desirable than the other. Instead, the diverse range of expression is the normal outcome of a healthy and vital native artistic community.

Both traditional and individualized contemporary jewelry styles are popular in the established worlds of Indian arts and high fashion today. They are displayed, worn, sold, and appraised side by side in many select galleries across the country. The two styles complement each other and add a greater variety to choices available for purchase by both native and non-native buyers of Indian jewelry. In turn, both styles of jewelry help to reinforce in the talented native artisans a greater sense of pride in their ancient traditions and in their abilities as individual artists in their own right. The two styles are different interpretations of a tradition that has incorporated and continues to blend prehistoric native culture with Spanish and Mexican and contemporary American themes to create an art form that is truly American in every sense.

This "new Indian" style ring is an example of the "corn row" or "ear of corn" inlay technique which the master Hopi artisan Charles Loloma first pioneered in the 1960's. Today, many different craftsmen are creating versions of this contemporary rendition of traditional mosaic inlay work. It draws its inspiration directly from prehistoric and early historic jewelry styles.

The Navajo silversmith Sam Yellowhorse set a cabochon of Pilot Mountain, Nevada, turquoise into this hand wrought silver cuff bracelet. The "new Indian" style of bracelet draws its inspiration from traditional ethnic styles modified by contemporary influences. The price code of a pawn broker is engraved along the inside edge at left.

Hopi overlay pin set with turquoise, ca. 1985. Few Hopi silversmiths use turquoise or other stones as accents in their jewelry. Instead, most prefer to work with the silver alone. This attractive example by Mark Lomayestewa nicely combines silver overlay with turquoise.

New Directions in Indian Jewelry 73

Four sterling silver belt buckles, ca. 1970's-1980's. The variously colored blue and green turquoise sets come from different mines and localities in the Southwest. These handsome buckles rest on a brightly colored Hopi wicker plaque and are examples of both traditional and modern styles.

This Navajo-style hand-stamped sterling concha belt was made by H. Henderson in the third quarter of the 20th century.

Gallery of Indian Jewelry

"American Indians are our only true American artists, our real cultural heritage, an incredible creative force that have been a very real source of inspiration to the fortunate few who have made Indian art part of their living experience."
—*Vincent Price, actor and former director of the Indian Arts and Crafts Board*

Belts

These four Navajo belts are draped across a late 19th century Navajo twill-weave saddle blanket. They include, from right to left: a Navajo-style silver overlay buckle by F. Wero that sports three large nuggets of Kingman seafoam turquoise, a Navajo belt with hand cast conchas and butterfly spacers, a classic-style Navajo concha belt hand wrought by Roger Skeet, Jr., and a Navajo hand wrought buckle with central turquoise cabochon and stamped designs, on a belt studded with domed buffalo nickels.

In the late 19th century photograph, the Navajo Gayetenito and his wife are wearing traditional examples of early Indian jewelry. Early examples also include a heishi necklace with turquoise joclas and several ketohs. The ketohs illustrated here include a late 19th to early 20th century Navajo-style hand wrought example (top), an early to mid-20th century Navajo-style cast example (center), and a Zuni-style hand wrought ketoh (front) with embossed butterfly ornaments that dates to about 1930. The turquoise stone in the Zuni ketoh is a recent replacement for an earlier stone or carved fetish.

Large belt of sterling silver with closed-center conchas and butterfly spacers. This belt was made within the past 15 years but is modelled on a classic belt which the Navajo smith Hosteen Goodluck fashioned in 1929 for a major collector and Indian trader at Zuni, named C. G. Wallace.

These assorted concha belts are only a small sampling of work by Navajo, Zuni, Hopi, and Pueblo smiths. While the range of styles and techniques has expanded in recent years, the popularity of this traditional belt has remained constant for more than a century. (Photo by Ted Hill, courtesy of Gilbert Ortega Galleries of Fine Indian Arts.)

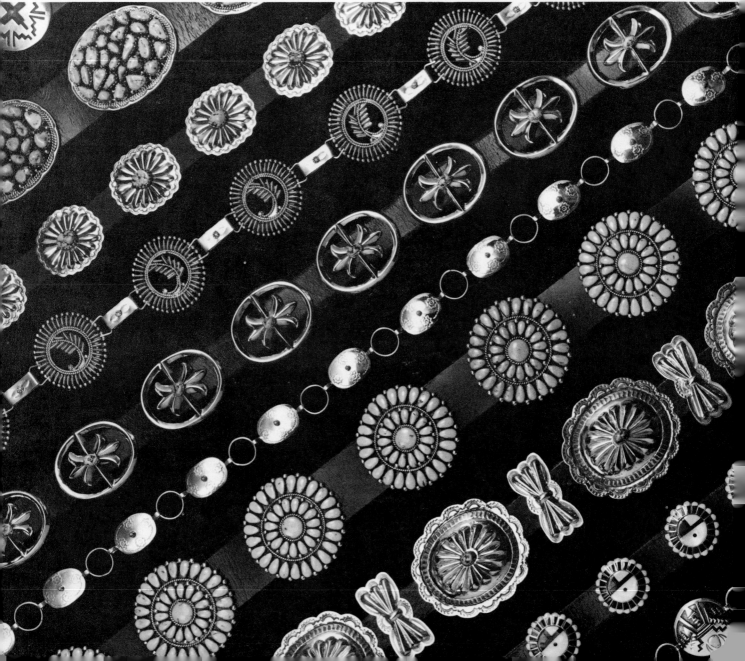

Bracelets

The Navajo word for "bracelet" is "LaTsini." These assorted single-stone cuff bracelets illustrate some of the 20th century styles that the Navajo create. Navajo craftsmen traditionally emphasize the silver and use turquoise only to set off the designs of their silver pieces. Usually, these designs are balanced, symmetrical, or repetitive. The lyre pattern of the silverwork on the bracelet in the foreground, for example, is balanced with a large central stone of turquoise. The twisted wire bezel is embellished further with four silver applique leaf elements and silver drops.

Two tourist-era bracelets. The embossed example (left) is probably the earlier of the two bracelets.

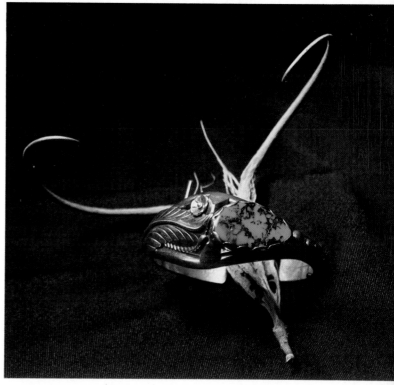

This attractive contemporary bracelet, signed "FP," encircles a devil's claw (Martynia) seedpod used to make black designs in some native Southwestern baskets. High-quality Bisbee turquoise and silver applique are combined to make this unusual piece.

Large Navajo cuff bracelet and matching ring, early 1970's. The mosaic inlay by Navajo artisan T. Begay is of mother-of-pearl, jet, turquoise, and coral. The figure is an Apache ghan (Mountain Spirit) dancer who plays a role in girls' puberty ceremonies. The wrought silverwork of the bracelet is by a second Navajo craftsman.

Hopi silver overlay cuff bracelet, ca. 1985. Stylized animal paw and feather design elements accent this slender cuff bracelet.

Zuni smiths typically create the silver frame for a piece of jewelry and then shape the turquoise stones to set into the bezels. On occasion, the Zuni will buy the completed silver frames from Navajo smiths and then will set their turquoise stones into them. This lovely bracelet is an example of Zuni-style "petit-point" cluster lapidary, which today is popular among both Zuni and Navajo peoples. The silverwork for this especially large example was fashioned by Navajo artisan M. Begay.

Necklaces

avajo-style necklace of handmade beads with four
utterflies and a naja, ca. 1935. The handcast naja is
t with turquoise from the Cerrillos mines, south of
nta Fe, New Mexico. These mines have been
orked since prehistoric times. The back of the
cklace—the section that would rest against the
pe of the neck—is finished off with the traditional
squaw wrap" binding of string or cord, instead of
ith a clasp.

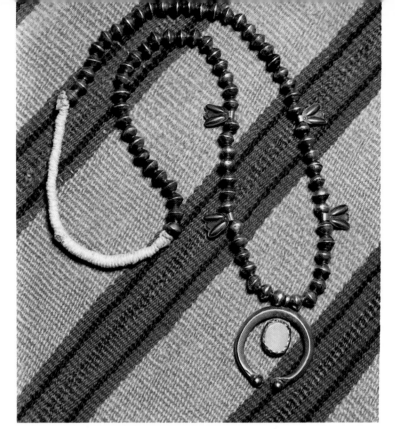

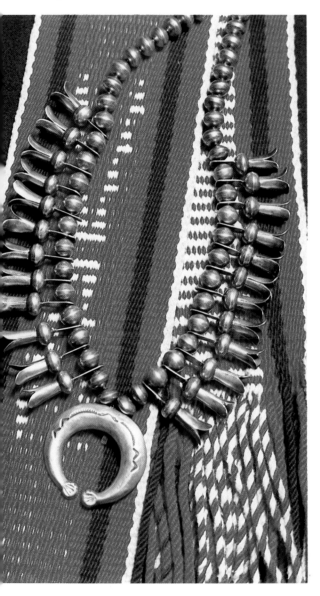

This silver Navajo-style naja with hands is strung on
machine-made round beads and melon or pinyon
beads, early 1980's. The crescent-shaped naja is an
ancient design element. During Roman times, it
served as a charm to ward off the Evil Eye. The
crescent eventually was adopted by the Moors of
northern Africa and then by the Spanish. They, in
turn, brought the naja to Mexico and the Southwest
where they used it as an ornament on the headstalls
of horse bridles. Early Navajo smiths quickly
adopted the attractive crescent. Hands forming the
ends of the naja were being made by the close of the
19th century and have continued to be a popular
adaptation of the simple crescent design throughout
the 20th century.

he Navajo word for "squash blossom necklace" is
Yoo nimazi." This necklace has hand wrought
quash blossoms and beads as well as a hand cast
aja. The necklace is made in the style of Ambrose
oanhorse (1904-1982), a Navajo smith known for
is elegantly simple compositions and techniques.
oanhorse used hand-made dies and also embossed,
hased, and filed his forms. This necklace rests
gainst a colorful Navajo dance sash from the 1930's.

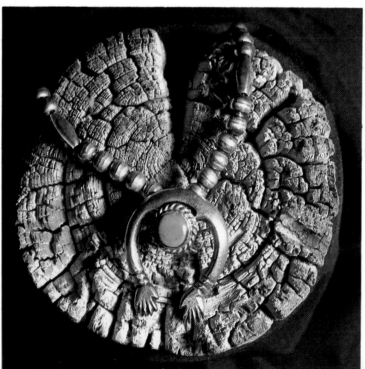

Navajo squash blossom necklace, ca. 1970's. The silver naja and trumpet-like blossoms of this attractive necklace are set with beautiful green turquoise from the Manassa mine in southern Colorado.

This Navajo necklace, ca. 1970, combines silver overlay with chip inlay of turquoise and coral. Different widths of the bird beaks and slight variations in body contours, as well as differences in decorative inlay and tooling of the silver show that the water bird (or anhinga) pendants on this necklace are entirely hand-made.

Navajo cast silver naja, ca. 1975. The fleur d'lis terminals and accent of red Mediterranean coral create a graceful variation on the typical naja form. The fleur d'lis design element has been popular among native Southwestern Indians because of its resemblance to the corn plant.

...e world's largest squash blossom necklace weighs ...ore than 40 pounds and features old Bisbee ...quoise. The necklace was made in Gallup, New ...xico, and, according to Gilbert Ortega Galleries ...Fine Indian Arts, it is said to have been worn by ...ted celebrities including King Kong, the Hulk, ...d the Jolly Green Giant! (Photo by George C. ...ght, courtesy of Gilbert Ortega Galleries of Fine ...lian Arts.)

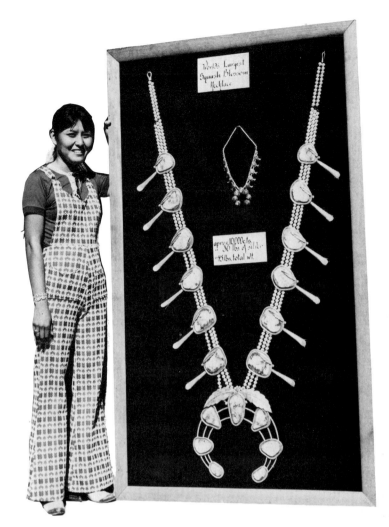

...gle strand of Navajo handmade silver beads, early ...0's. Decorations on the larger beads are stamped. ...ndmade silver beads are highly treasured on the ...ervations. They are seldom pawned because they ... so time-consuming to make.

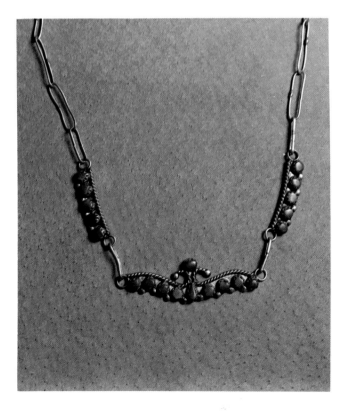

...all Zuni collar with handmade chain and round ...etitpoint" lapidary, occasionally called "snake ...s." When buying Zuni jewelry, a customer is ...entially paying only for the labor used to make the ...ce; considerably more labor than silver or ...quoise usually is put into their jewelry.

A Santo Domingo Pueblo tab necklace with shell heishi and a pair of jocla rests on fossilized ripple marks left by an ancient sea. Both women and men originally wore the "jocla," Navajo for "ear string," as earrings which were hung from the necklace when not in use. Artisans living in the Rio Grande pueblos, such as Santo Domingo, have traded handmade turquoise and shell beads to the Navajo and Zuni for generations.

Turquoise and shell necklace with joclas. This necklace includes several styles of handmade beads. The tapered white shell beads at the bottom of each jocla resemble corn kernels and are referred to as "corn." The hand rolled turquoise and brown olivella shell beads are called "heishi." The red beads at the top of each jocla are glass trade beads in this example, although beads of coral or spiny oyster shell may be used. The square-shaped turquoise tab beads of graduated sizes are both unusual and attractive. All represent considerable effort on the part of the maker.

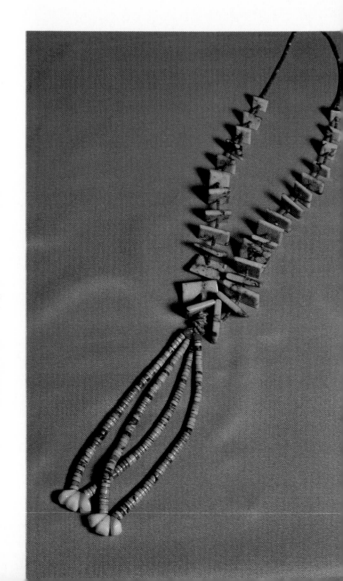

Red coral from the Mediterranean has been a very popular material among Indian craftsmen since its first modern-day importation to the Zuni in 1936. It is red—a sacred color for the Zuni—and is thought to bring the wearer good luck and longevity. As illustrated here, coral may be shaped for use in silverwork as in the "shadowbox" applique style cuff bracelet, or it may be drilled to be worn in strands. This jewelry is featured against whalebone and a fossil shell called ammonite.

Two native crosses, ca. 1970's. Silver crosses have long been popular among Southwestern peoples. These two examples serve as pendants on necklaces of red trade beads. The larger "green heart" (ca. 1600-1775) cornaline d'Aleppo beads are earlier than the "white heart" variety which was made into the early 19th century.

Ceremonial jewelry is rarely seen off of the reservations. Yet, it does exist and is culturally significant. This silver overlay necklace is associated with the Peyote Cult. The pendant on this hand wrought wrapped-link chain has a complex and meaningful design. It includes a human face, a sacred corn plant, and an anhinga or water bird. An inverted button holds a six-strand tassel of brain-tanned leather. The silver chain incorporates thirteen red mescal beans. The peyote waterbird style of jewelry has been popular since about 1890. It relates directly to peyote ceremonialism associated with the Native American religion found among some Indian groups of the Great Plains and Southwest.

Necklaces 83

Pins

Navajo-style cluster pin or pendant. Though th cluster work technique resembles its Zuni counter part, the free-form shape of these turquoise sets i more typical of Navajo than Zuni small stone work This article, as are many, is made to be worn either a a pin or as a pendant.

This six-inch long silver "eagle" or "thunderbird" pin is decorated with a busy array of interesting stampwork, some chiselwork, and repousse emboss- ing. The tourist-era piece dates probably to the late 1920's.

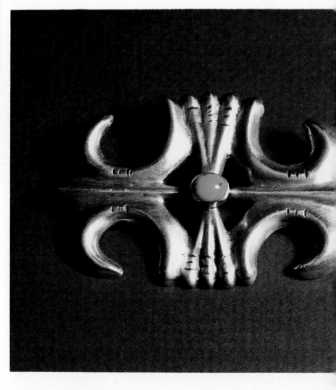

Navajo hand cast brooch, ca. 1970's. Decorative chiselwork and a turquoise cabochon finish off the polished cast silverwork.

These three Zuni-style cluster pins suggest the range of variation that exists in this type of jewelry. The two round pins are by T. Mutte, the larger oval example is signed "OQ."

Three Hopi overlay pins, ca. 1985. Hopi silversmiths have used tiny jigsaws to cut out the naturalistic and stylized designs in the top layer of silver. After blackening the surface of a second sheet of silver, they have soldered together the two silver layers. In Hopi overlay, the blackened background is textured with distinctive stampwork.

Hopi overlay pin, ca. 1985. Many Hopi silversmiths draw their inspiration from nature. This stylized silver paw closely resembles the paw of a black bear.

Rings

Two Navajo-style rings, early 1980's. Shadowbox applique silverwork and turquoise are combined to create these attractive accessories.

More than 20 assorted rings lend a splash of color to tiers of cactus wood. Stones used in silverwork include: turquoise, chrysocolla, coral, and dark blue lapis lazuli. Various techniques have been employed to shape and set these stones. The ring at the upper left represents the "whirling logs" motif, a common good luck symbol prior to the 1930's.

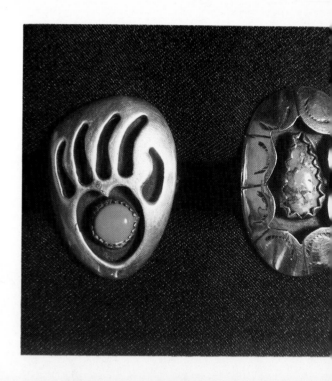

Navajo man's ring. This massive ring is sculpted from heavy silver which frames an oval cabochon of turquoise.

Navajo chip inlay ring, early 1970's. A chip inlay hummingbird hovers over a nectar-filled flower on this attractive Navajo silver ring with stamped border design. This ring bears the hallmark of "J.W."

Three Navajo long rings, ca. 1965-1975. The center ring of this elegant trio measures about three inches in length! All are displayed against a pottery seed jar which was made at Acoma Pueblo.

Assorted Jewelry Styles

Turquoise-encrusted silver watch bands are popular both on and off the reservations. These examples include a Navajo man's watch with decorative silver applique and pillbox closure (upper left), a Navajo turquoise cluster cuff-bracelet-type watch (upper right), a Navajo woman's cuff-bracelet-style watch with three natural seafoam turquoise nuggets from the Kingman mine (lower left), and a Zuni watch with round "snake eye" petitpoint turquoise sets.

Carved turquoise usually is created only by Zuni artists. Here, travertine that formed in a western hot spring supports various life forms in turquoise. The upper left sports a ring of carved turquoise and silver leaves above several pairs of earrings. Bluebirds created by Zuni fetish carver David Tsikewa shortly before his death in 1970 nest below worked turquoise scallop shells and petitpoint flowerettes. Three blue frogs, mounted in a cast silver cuff, peek out from below.

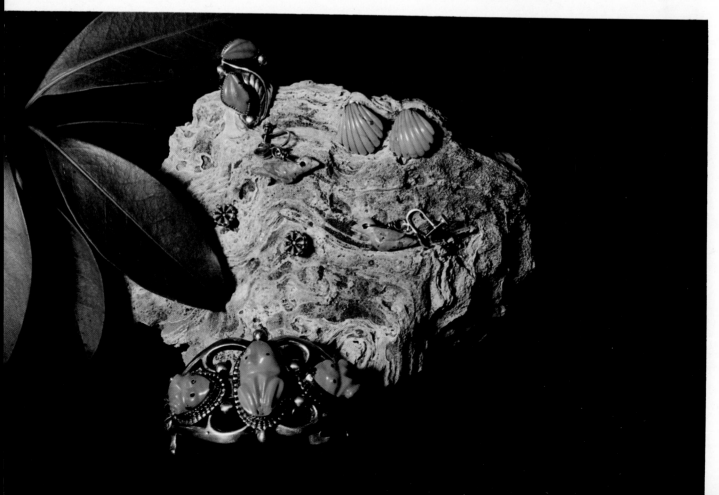

Men's bolo tie slides, ca. 1970's. They are, from left to right: Navajo "wedding basket design" overlay silver and copper slide with miniature baskets dangling from the tips, Zuni turquoise "petitpoint" cluster slide on a black thong of braided leather, and a Navajo silver overlay slide. Indian-made bolo tie slides first were made in about 1950 and enjoy considerable popularity in the West.

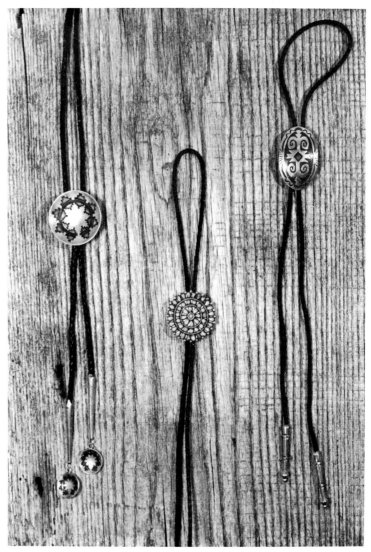

Hat band purchased from a Navajo Indian from Farmington, New Mexico, early 1980's. Fashioned with a tasteful combination of white and black horsehair, this hat band is decorated with seven ornamental tooled silver bands.

A Navajo smith living near Farmington, New Mexico, created this hair barrette in the mid 1980's. The style of hair ornament is a comparatively new form, although the design and decorative die stamping on the turtle-like silver form looks traditional.

Navajo or Hopi style "squash blossom" hair ornaments, ca. 1940-1960. Silver chopstick hairpins were first made after about 1940, but virtually no early silver hairpins have been seen off of the reservations since the late 1960's, according to Charles Eagle Plume of Colorado. Today, many native women use plastic or store-bought metal styles, instead.

Glossary

APPLIQUE—A decorative technique in which silver cut-outs, such as leaves or feathers, are soldered to an article of silver jewelry.

CAST—A technique of forming handmade silver jewelry that uses molten silver and a mold of tufa, sandstone, concrete or other material.

CLUSTER—A term used to describe Zuni-style small stone work. A group of small, shaped stones that are set close together in individual silver bezels.

COIN SILVER—Metal with silver content of about .900 purity. Jewelry made from melted coins in the 19th century is also referred to as "coin silver."

CONCHA—From the Spanish word for "shell." An oval or round metal disc, usually with scalloped edges, that is found on some belts, pins, bolo ties, and other articles of jewelry.

FETISH—Any natural or man-made object, usually in the shape of an animal, bird, or other life form, in which a spirit is believed to dwell.

FILEWORK—A technique which uses a file for smoothing or finishing silver. A file also can be used to make decorative lines or marks on silver.

FINE SILVER—Metal with a silver content of .999 purity.

GERMAN SILVER or NICKEL SILVER—An alloy of copper, nickel, and zinc with no precious metal content. This alloy visually resembles sterling silver and is used in less expensive jewelry.

HALLMARK—Maker's mark. Southwestern Indian makers' marks consist of cast, engraved, or stamped names, initials, or symbols, usually located on the reverse of a piece of jewelry.

HEISHI—The Santo Domingo word for "shell," this term refers to fine, hand-rolled beads of shell, turquoise, coral, or other materials generally made in the Rio Grande pueblos.

INLAY—A technique in which a decorative stone or mosaic is set into silver or shell so that it is flush with the surface.

JOCLA—Navajo for "earring," this term generally is used today to refer to the double loop of rolled turquoise beads that hang like a pendant from some turquoise and shell necklaces.

KACHINA—A stylized human form which is the symbolic representation of a spirit. Each kachina has specific stylized characteristics that make it readily recognizable. The Morning Singer Talavi, for example (see page 58), wears a special mask and head-dress all his own.

KETOH—Navajo for "bow guard" or maponi in Hopi. A wide leather band, usually with a decorative silver plate. It used to be worn like a bracelet on the left wrist to protect the wearer from the snap of the bow string. Today, the bow guard is worn primarily in ceremonial contexts.

MANTA PIN—A pin, usually of silver or turquoise and silver, which is worn at the shoulder to fasten a Pueblo woman's manta, or traditional dress.

MATRIX—Veins or spots of the rock in which turquoise is found that show up as markings in turquoise.

MOSAIC—A decorative technique in which small pieces of coral, shell, turquoise, or other stone form a design that is set into or onto an article of silver or shell.

NAJA—A Navajo word for the crescent-shaped pendant that hangs from silver bridles, squash blossom necklaces, and other jewelry articles.

NEEDLEPOINT—A type of small stone cluster work which uses stones that are long, thin, and pointed at both ends.

NICKEL SILVER—see German silver.

OVERLAY—A technique of silverworking in which two sheets of silver are soldered together after first cutting out a design in the top layer. This technique was first practiced among the Hopi.

OXIDIZE—To blacken silver deliberately with a chemical reagent in order to create greater contrast or to accent a silverwork design.

PAWN—An object with monetary worth, such as a piece of jewelry, a saddle, or a gun, which is held by a trader or pawn broker as collateral for a loan of cash.

PETITPOINT—A type of small stone cluster work which uses stones that are round, oval, or teardrop in shape. Petitpoint with completely round stones is sometimes referred to as "snake eyes."

REPOUSSE—A decorative technique in which hand-wrought silver is hammered from the reverse side to create embossed or raised, dome-like designs.

SQUASH BLOSSOM—A silver bead, occasionally embellished with turquoise or other materials, that has petals attached and represents the pomegranate blossom.

STABILIZE—To treat turquoise with a resin, plastic, oil or other substance to give it greater hardness. Dye may be added at the same time to heighten the color of a pale stone.

STAMPWORK—A decorative technique which uses small metal punches similar to leather tooling punches to stamp designs into silver.

STERLING SILVER—Metal with silver content of .925 purity alloyed with .075 copper to make it harder.

TURQUOISE—A semiprecious stone, hydrous aluminum phosphate, with a hardness of Moh 5-6. Copper salts give the stone its distinctive blue-green color.

WROUGHT—A technique of forming handmade silver jewelry that involves the hammering out of silver into a desired shape.

For Further Reading

Adair, John. 1944. **The Navajo and Pueblo Silversmiths.** University of Oklahoma Press. Norman, OK. *A standard introduction to the topic.*

Bahti, Mark. 1980. **Collecting Southwestern Native American Jewelry.** David McKay Company, Inc. New York, NY.

Bahti, Tom. 1983. **Southwestern Indian Arts and Crafts** (revised edition). K.C. Publications. Las Vegas, NV.

Bedinger, Marjorie. 1973. **Indian Silver: Navajo and Pueblo Jewelers.** University of New Mexico Press. Albuquerque, NM. *In-depth history of Indian jewelry making.*

Bell, Barbara, and Edward Bell. 1975. **Zuni, the Art and the People: Zuni Silversmiths** (3 vol.). Squaw Bell Traders. Grants, NM. *Biographical sketches and photos of many contemporary craftsmen.*

Branson, Oscar T. 1975. **Turquoise: The Gem of the Centuries.** Treasure Chest Publications, Inc. Tucson, AZ. *Useful in identifying turquoise from different mines.*

_____. 1977. **Indian Jewelry Making, Vol. 1 and 2.** Treasure Chest Publications, Inc. Tucson, AZ. *A how-to book with much on the techniques.*

Conroy, Kathleen. 1975. **What You Should Know about Authentic Indian Jewelry.** Gro-Pub Group. Denver, CO.

Cooper, Tom C. (ed.). 1979. Collector's Edition—The New Look in Indian Jewelry. **Arizona Highways.** Vol. 55, No. 4. Phoenix, AZ.

Frank, Larry, and Millard J. Holbrook, II. 1978. **Indian Silver Jewelry of the Southwest, 1868-1930.** New York Graphic Society. New York, NY. *Colorfully illustrated history of Classic style jewelry.*

Hammack, Nancy S., and Jerry Jacka. 1975. **Indian Jewelry of the Prehistoric Southwest.** University of Arizona Press. Tucson, AZ. *A colorful introduction to the topic.*

Jacka, Jerry, and Spencer Gill. 1975. **Turquoise Treasures.** Graphic Arts Center Publishing Co. Portland, OR.

Jernigan, Wesley. 1976. **Jewelry of the Prehistoric Southwest.** University of New Mexico Press. Albuquerque, NM. *A detailed and scholarly treatise.*

King, Dale Stuart. 1976. **Indian Silverwork of the Southwest, Vol. 2.** Dale Stuart King. Tucson, AZ. (For Vol. 1, see Mera 1977.)

Lincoln, Louise (ed.). 1982. **Southwest Indian Silver from the Doneghy Collection.** University of Texas Press. Austin, TX. *Documents an extensive personal collection now in the Minneapolis Institute of Arts.*

Mera, Harry P. 1977. **Indian Silverwork of the Southwest, Illustrated.** Dale Stuart King. Tucson, AZ. (Reprint of 1959 edition.)

Neumann, David L. 1971. **Navajo Silverwork.** Museum of New Mexico Press. Santa Fe, NM.

Rosnek, Carl, and Joseph Stacey. 1976. **Skystone and Silver: The Collector's Book of Southwest Indian Jewelry.** Prentice-Hall, Inc. Englewood Cliffs, NJ.

Stacey, Joseph (ed.). 1975. **Turquoise Blue Book and Indian Jewelry Digest.** Arizona Highways. Phoenix, AZ. *A compilation of three popular special jewelry collectors' issues of* **Arizona Highways** *magazine.*

Tanner, Clara Lee. 1968. **Southwest Indian Craft Arts.** University of Arizona Press. Tucson, AZ.

Woodward, Arthur. 1971. **Navajo Silver: A Brief History of Navajo Silversmithing.** Northland Press. Flagstaff, AZ. (Reprint of 1938 edition.)

Wright, Margaret. 1982. **Hopi Silver: The History and Hallmarks of Hopi Silversmithing** (third edition). Northland Press. Flagstaff, AZ. *Includes hallmarks of most Hopi smiths.*

Price Guide

"If you compare high quality Indian jewelry with other silver jewelry anywhere, Indian jewelry is still the best buy in the world."—Joe Tanner, Tanner's Indian Arts Gallery.

The prices of Indian jewelry vary widely. They depend upon the age and condition of a piece, the geographic location of the market, the type of shop—ranging from a native vendor or outdoor market to a shop or gallery, the reputation and name of the maker, the quality and size of turquoise or other stones, the weight and craftsmanship of the silver, and the complexity and aesthetic appeal of the design. The prices provided here are currently found in today's average jewelry shops and galleries, when sterling silver is trading for about $6.50 an ounce. Prices often will vary greatly from one outlet to the next, and they also may change at any time with the fluctuating price of silver. While a potential buyer must make his or her own final decision on a piece, this list may serve as a guide.

Barrettes

Navajo, tooled silver	$35
Zuni, petitpoint turquoise or coral	$40

Belt buckles

Navajo, silver overlay with 1 stone	$75—100
Navajo, silver overlay with 3 stones	$150—250
Zuni, nugget style in silver	$185
Zuni, turquoise channel inlay	$275—600
Zuni, multicolor channel inlay	$230—400

Bolo ties

Hopi, silver overlay	$80—300
Navajo, nugget style in silver	$200
Zuni, multicolor inlay	$90—175
Zuni, multicolor channel inlay	$160—275
Zuni, turquoise channel inlay	$225—625

Bow guards (ketoh or maponi)

Hopi maponi, silver overlay	$350
Navajo ketoh, wrought silver with 1 stone	$175—800
Navajo ketoh, cast silver with 1 stone	$300—650
Zuni bow guard, multicolor inlay	$425

Bracelets

Hopi, narrow cuff, silver overlay	$30—60
Hopi, medium cuff, silver overlay	$60—150
Hopi, wide cuff, silver overlay	$85 and up
Navajo, narrow cuff, silver applique	$40—65
Navajo, three-wire cuff, 1 stone	$50—200
Navajo, heavy wrought cuff, 1 stone	$50—350
Navajo, cuff, wrought silver, no stones	$45—175
Navajo, cuff, cast silver with or without stone	$30—350
Zuni, bangle, simple petitpoint	$20—40
Zuni, link bracelet, clusterwork or inlay	$40—125
Zuni, cuff, inlay and channel "sunface" kachina	$250—310
Zuni, narrow cuff, turquoise clusterwork	$50—70
Zuni, medium cuff, turquoise clusterwork	$90—125
Zuni, narrow cuff, turquoise channelwork	$40
Zuni, medium cuff, channelwork	$90—280
Zuni, wide cuff, intricate turquoise needlepoint	$475
Zuni, wide cuff, 12 large turquoise nuggets	$850

Buttons

Navajo, handcut and tooled silver	$10—45 ea.

Concha belts

Hopi, silver overlay	$1800
Navajo, small, silver conchas with 1 stone	$130—450
Navajo, small child's sandcast silver conchas and butterflies	$300
Navajo, large, 11 conchas or 6 conchas with 5 butterflies	$500—3500
Zuni, large, turquoise petitpoint	$2400

Cufflinks

Navajo, nugget style, 1 stone	$60
Zuni, multicolor inlay	$120

Earrings

Hopi, silver overlay, small stud	$10—30
Hopi, silver overlay, large stud	$40—90
Hopi, silver overlay, drops of various shapes	$30—90
Navajo, small turquoise studs	$5—15
Navajo, silver applique leaves	$20
Navajo, silver studs or buttons	$20—35
Santo Domingo Pueblo, mosaic inlay on spiny oyster shell drops	$20—45
Santo Domingo Pueblo, jocla-style drops	$25—45
Zuni, small turquoise studs	$8—12
Zuni, channel, inlay, or cluster turquoise studs	$20—50
Zuni, channel, inlay, or cluster drops (average)	$15—60
Zuni, turquoise needlepoint (large)	$125
Zuni, turquoise clusterwork drop (large)	$115

Hair combs

Zuni, set of two, turquoise clusterwork	$40—90

Key Chains

Zuni, multicolor inlay	$50
Zuni, multicolor "sunface" inlay	$45

Money clips

Zuni, multicolor kachina inlay	$30
Zuni, multicolor "sunface" inlay	$35
Zuni, nugget-style turquoise, 1 stone	$40

Necklaces

Hopi, silver overlay, three-piece choker	$150—400
Hopi, silver overlay, 2-sided pendant on handmade silver chain	$250
Jocla necklaces (various tribes)	$60—700
Navajo, silver squash blossom necklace	$200—750
Navajo, silver and turquoise squash blossom necklaces	$200—3000
Cochiti Pueblo, heishi and bird fetish necklace, 2 strands	$150
Cochiti Pueblo, heishi and turquoise nugget necklace, 2 strands	$50
San Felipe Pueblo, 5-strand heishi and turquoise choker with removable pendant	$200
Santo Domingo Pueblo, 16" nugget necklace	$50

Santo Domingo, pendant, mosaic inlay on spiny oyster shell	$60—125
Santo Domingo, large turquoise tabs and heishi necklace	$200
Santo Domingo, sandcast silver pendant with coral and turquoise by Harold Lovato	$200
Zuni, fetish and heishi necklace	$125 per strand
Zuni, turquoise fetish necklace	$275 per strand
Zuni, turquoise petitpoint choker w/earrings	$170—200
Zuni, turquoise channelwork choker w/earrings	$60—380
Zuni, turquoise needlepoint choker w/earrings	$140—550
Zuni, turquoise needlepoint squash blossom	$1050
Zuni, inlay choker w/handmade chain	$165
Zuni, inlay "sunface" choker w/handmade chain	$150
Zuni, inlay pendant on handmade chain	$100
Zuni, inlay pendant on strand of silver beads	$250

Pins/pendants

Hopi, silver overlay w/turquoise, large	$75—150
Hopi, silver overlay, medium	$25—80
Navajo, turquoise, 1 stone, small	$25
Navajo, turquoise, 1 stone, large	$75
Navajo, silver applique leaves	$30
Navajo, petitpoint pin	$50—100
Navajo, naja pendant	$50—300
Navajo, silver cross pendant, large	$50—125
Navajo, silver and copper overlay, "wedding basket" pin	$25—60
Navajo, sandcast silver with 1 stone	$75
Zuni, turquoise petitpoint or channelwork, small	$20—25
Zuni, turquoise petitpoint, medium	$35—60
Zuni, turquoise petitpoint or cluster, large	$60—100
Zuni, turquoise needlepoint, large	$90—170
Zuni, multicolor kachina, channelwork, large	$150—250

Rings

Navajo, average single stone turquoise	$20—150
Navajo, silver applique leaves	$25
Navajo, turquoise clusterwork	$20—65
Zuni, channelwork or clusterwork, simple and small	$20—60
Zuni, channelwork or clusterwork, large	$35—180
Zuni, inlay kachina, large	$65—90
Zuni, carved turquoise figure	$35—75
Zuni, cast with 2 turquoise nuggets	$60—75
Zuni, men's turquoise channelwork, small	$35
Zuni, men's turquoise channelwork, large	$200

Stickpins

Zuni, petitpoint	$20
Zuni, inlay and channelwork "sunface"	$25—30
Zuni, complex turquoise channelwork	$90

Tie bars and tie tacks

Zuni, multicolor inlay, bar	$35
Zuni, multicolor inlay, tack	$20—45

Watches

Zuni, ladies' turquoise cluster watch tips	$50
Zuni, men's turquoise channelwork tips	$110
Zuni, ladies' multicolor inlay tips	$75—200
Zuni, ladies' multicolor channelwork tips	$75
Navajo, ladies' silver applique w/1 stone, tips	$35
Navajo, men's applique silver band w/2 stones	$50—300
Navajo, ladies' cuff with turquoise nuggets	$150
Navajo, ladies' cuff with turquoise clusterwork	$200—400

Index

Numerals in **boldface** type refer to photos and captions

A

Aguilar, Florence **16**
Albuquerque, NM 30, 68
Anasazi **5**, **9**, 10, **11**, **12**, **13**, 51, 65
Anea, Juan 43
Atencio, Ralph 67
Atsidi Chon **43**, 53, 61
Atsidi Sani 19, **43**
Aragon, Vidal **67**
Aztec, NM 11, 14

B

Bahti, Mark 36
Begay family 48, **78**
Belt, front cover, 24, 35, **36**, **37**, **42**, 44, 49, **54**, 74-76
Benally, Mary L. **54**
Blass, Bill 9
Bolo tie 45, 49, **89**
Boone, Alex and Marylita **57**
Boone, Lena **66**
Bow guard 15, 24, **25**, 44, 75
Bracelet **5**, **22**, 24, **25**, **27**, **32**, **34**, **43**, 44, **45**, 49, 51, **52**, **54**, **57**, **58**, 61, **71**, **72**, **73**, **77-78**, **88**
Butterfly spacer, see Belt
Buttons 24, **25**, **47**, **48**, 49

C

Carson, Kit 42
Carter, George 43
Casas Grandes, Mexico 11, **12**, 14
Cerrillos mines, NM **12**, 53, 68, **79**
Chaco Canyon, NM 11, **12**, 14
Clark, Carl **71**
Colton, Harold and Mary 62
Concha **34**, **43**
Coochwytewa, Victor **62**
Coral 68, 80, **83**
    tests for genuineness **32**
Coronado 14, 51
Cuff links 49

D

Dishta 54
Desyee, Leekya 54, **55**
Dress ornaments 48, 49

E

Eagle Plume, Charles **90**
Earrings **16**, 24, **27**, 49, 53, **54**, **57**, **60**, **61**, **63**, **88**
Edaakie, Lee 54

F

fish 55
agstaff, AZ **30**
ower, Manuelita **16**, 66, 67

G

allup, NM 68
ayetenito **75**
lbert Ortega Galleries **31**, **81**
oldwater, Barry M. 6
oodluck, Hosteen **70**, **76**

H

air ornaments 49, **90**
arvey, Fred **26**, **27**
alona, NM 51
at band **89**
awikuh, NM 52, 53, 54, **55**
eishi (see also Necklace) **64**, **66-69**, 82
enderson, H. **74**
odge, F. W. 52
ohokam 10, **11**, 14
opi 15, 23, 26, 58-63, 67, 72
opi Silvercraft Guild 62, **63**
orse equipment **15**, 18, 24, **25**, 49
ubbell, J. Lorenzo **22**, 23
ubbell Trading Post **31**

I—J

dian jewelry
  authenticity 30, 35, 44, 62
  beginnings 9-22
  buying 29-37
  care of 38-39
  Classic period 23-27
  coins, use of **22**, 23, 43, **48**, 49
  copper, use of 19, **27**, 34, **45**
  hallmarks **36-37**
  new directions 26, 29, 70-73
  Plains Indian influence **18**, **23**, 24, 26
  prehistory 5, 10-14, 61
  Spanish influence 15-19, 24, 26, **40**
  techniques **20**, **21**, 34, 43
  tourist-era 25, 26, **27**, 77, **84**
nstitute of American Indian Arts 72
ocla **42**, **64**, 68, **75**, 82

K

abotie, Fred **71**
achina 50, **56**, **58**, **91**
eneshde 53
etoh (see Bow guard)
ey chain 49
irk, Dean **45**

L

anyade 43, 53, 61
eki, Edna **55**
oloma, Charles 62, 71, **73**
omayestewa, Mark **73**
ovato, Harold **36**, **72**
ummis, Charles (quoted) 65

M

ansfield, Vernon **37**, **61**
ason, James **47**
assif, J. D. **56**
esa Verde, CO **10**, **11**, **13**

Moenkopi, AZ 59
Mogollon 5, 10, **11**, 51
Money clip 49
Monongye, Preston 26, 62, **63**, 71
Museum of Northern Arizona 62
Mutte, T. **front cover**, **85**

N

Naja pendant 40, **79**
Natewa, B. **51**
Navajo **17**, **18**, **19**, **20**, 23, 25, 26, **29**, 34, 35, 40-49, 67, 68, **71**, 72
Necklace **front cover**, 4, 5, **16**, **17**, **22**, 24, **25**, 32, 35, **36**, **37**, 40, 42, 46, 49, 50, 53, 54, 56, 57, **60**, **61**, **62**, **63**, **64**, **66**, **67**, **68**, **69**, **70**, **71**, **72**, 75, ·79-83
Needlepoint 53
Nizto, Dave and Celia 57

O

Oraibi, AZ 59, **60**
Ortega, Gilbert **31**
Oshki, Juan 54

P—Q

Papago 10
Pataiyan **11**
Pawn 28, 37, **38**, **39**
Paya, B. **45**
Peshlakai Atsidi **42**, 43
Petitpoint 53
Petrified wood 33
Peyote cult **83**
Pima 10, **61**
Pin **front cover**, 24, **34**, **35**, **37**, **45**, **47**, 49, **52**, **53**, **61**, **73**, **84-85**
Platero 19, 23
Platero, Fannie **46**
Price, Vincent (quoted) 75
Pueblo Bonito, NM **11**, **12**
Pueblo Revolt 15
Puebloans 10, 15, **16**, **17**, 18, 23, 26, **43**, 64-69
Quintana, Joseph and Jerry 66-67

R

Richardson Trading Company **31**
Ramoncito, Roman 53
Ramos, Diego 66
Reano, Charlotte **16**
Ring 9, **18**, 24, **27**, 32, 37, **45**, 47, 49, 51, 54, 61, **67**, **73**, **78**, **86-87**, **88**
Roanhorse, Ambrose **79**
Rosetta family 68
Rosnek, Carl (quoted) 59

S

Santa Fe, NM 9, **12**, 30, 53, 68, **79**
Santa Fe trail 19
Scottsdale, AZ 9
Seven Cities of Cibola 15, 51, 52
Sichomovi, AZ **30**
Sikyatala 61
Silver
  classification 34
  substitutes 34, 49
  techniques of working 23, **34**, **35**, 43, 44
  tests for fineness 34

Singer, Tom 45
Skeet, Roger, Jr. **front cover**, 75
Snaketown, AZ **10**, **11**, 14
Spincast 35, 44, 62
Squash blossom bead **40**

T—U—V

Tanner, Joe (quoted) 93
Techniques, metal-working 15, 24, 46, 66
  casting 35, 44, **72**, 84
  hammering 34, 43
  overlay 45, 58-63, **65**, 67, **72**, 85
Techniques, shell- and stone-working 10
  bead making 10, 64, **66**, 68
  carving 10, 15, 52, 54, **55**, **66**
  clusterwork 29, 47, 50, **52**, 53, **57**, 84, 85
  mosaic inlay 10, 15, **16**, 45, 52, 54, 56, **57**, 72, 73
Thomas, Richard 46
Tie tack 49
Tobe Turpen Trading Company **28**, **39**, **57**
Trade goods, European 19, 24, **83**
Trade routes, prehistoric 11, 14, **16**, **17**
Tsikewa, David and Mary 54, **88**
Turquoise
  care of 38
  defined 32-33
  first use with silver 23, 43
  prehistoric use 10-14
  sources **12**, 23, 29
  substitutes 33
  tests for genuineness 33

W

Wallace, C. G. **76**
Walpi, AZ **59**
Ward, Bob (quoted) 29
Watch band 49, **88**
Weake, Teddy 54
Wero, F. **75**
White Eagle 44
Wright, Barton 36
Wright, Margaret 36

X—Y—Z

Yellowhorse, Sam **73**
Zuni 10, 15, 18, 19, 23, **25**, 26, 29, 50-57, 67, 72
Zuni, Benjamin, Jr. 50
Zuni Craftsman Cooperative 56

Photo by Douglas C. Gamage

About the Authors

William A. Turnbaugh is Professor of Anthropology at the University of Rhode Island in Kingston, where he has been teaching since 1974. An archaeologist with research interests in the North American Indian, Dr. Turnbaugh is a graduate of Lycoming College and Harvard University, where he received his Ph.D. in Anthropology in 1973. Fieldwork has taken him to the Near East, Arctic Canada, Rocky Mountain West, and Northeastern United States.

Co-author Sarah Peabody Turnbaugh is Curator of the Museum of Primitive Culture in Peace Dale and Adjunct Assistant Professor of Anthropology at the University of Rhode Island. A Phi Beta Kappa graduate in Anthropology from Harvard and Radcliffe Colleges, she also holds a Master of Science degree in Textiles, Clothing and Related Arts from the University of Rhode Island.

The Turnbaughs are the authors of several other books including *Indian Baskets* (Schiffer). They live on Narragansett Bay in southern Rhode Island and travel regularly to museums, archaeological sites, and American Indian reservations and cultural centers throughout the United States and Canada.

Barry M. Goldwater, former U.S. Senator from Arizona and 1964 Republican nominee for President, provided the Foreword. He also is a long-time collector of Indian arts. His superb collection of Hopi kachinas is now permanently exhibited at the Heard Museum in Phoenix.

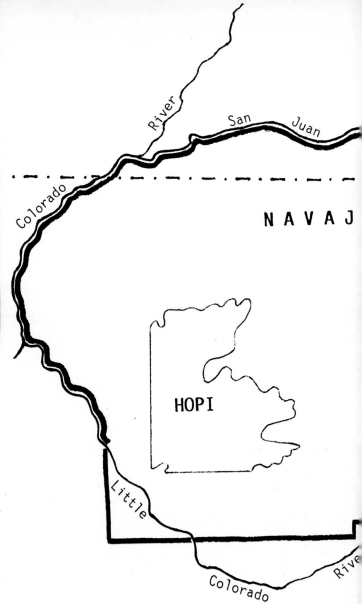

Locations of Indian Tribes and Reservations
Mentioned in the Text